New Paths and Policies towards Conflict Prevention

Chinese and Swiss Perspectives

T0347862

This book explores the discourse on conflict prevention and peace-building by bringing together researchers from China and Switzerland over a series of policy dialogues.

The Charter of the United Nations, adopted in the immediate aftermath of World War II, is clear about the fundamental necessity for the international community to act in partnership to prevent violent conflict. Given recent shifts in global power dynamics, there is an apparent need for international policy issues to be addressed in ways that are inclusive of a wider variety of perspectives and approaches. Chinese policy actors are increasingly interested in fostering their own discourse on issues of prevention and peacebuilding, rooted in Chinese experience, and engaging with peers from other contexts. The chapters in this volume explore the rationale for conflict prevention and review prevailing academic and practitioner discourses on fundamental questions such as why conflicts should be prevented and whether "mainstream approaches" are still relevant.

This book will be of interest to students of peacebuilding, conflict resolution, Chinese politics, and International Relations.

Courtney J. Fung is Assistant Professor of International Relations at The University of Hong Kong.

Björn Gehrmann is a German Diplomat and Mediator, who worked for the Human Security Division of the Swiss Federal Department of Foreign Affairs from 2017 to 2019.

Rachel F. Madenyika is UN Representative at the Quaker United Nations Office in New York, USA.

Jason G. Tower directs the Burma program of the United States Institute of Peace. (Formerly Southeast Asia Regional Advisor, PeaceNexus Foundation, Yangon.)

Series: Studies in Conflict, Development and Peacebuilding
Series Editors: Keith Krause, Oliver Jütersonke and Riccardo Bocco,
Centre on Conflict, Development and Peacebuilding (CCDP),
Graduate Institute, Switzerland

This series publishes innovative research into the connections between insecurity and under-development in fragile states, and into situations of violence and insecurity more generally.

It adopts a multidisciplinary approach to the study of a variety of issues, including the changing nature of contemporary armed violence (*conflict*), efforts to foster the conditions that prevent the outbreak or recurrence of such violence (*development*), and strategies to promote peaceful relations on the communal, societal and international level (*peacebuilding*).

Peacebuilding and Spatial Transformation
Peace, Space and Place
Annika Björkdahl and Stefanie Kappler

Exploring Peace Formation
Security and Justice in Post-Colonial States
Edited by Kwesi Aning, M. Anne Brown, Volker Boege, and Charles T. Hunt

Urban Safety and Peacebuilding
New Perspectives on Sustaining Peace in the City
Edited by Edited by Achim Wennmann and Oliver Jütersonke

New Paths and Policies towards Conflict Prevention
Chinese and Swiss Perspectives
Edited by Courtney J. Fung, Björn Gehrmann, Rachel F. Madenyika, and Jason G. Tower

For more information about this series, please visit: www.routledge.com/Studies-in-Conflict-Development-and-Peacebuilding/book-series/CONDEVPEACE

New Paths and Policies towards Conflict Prevention

Chinese and Swiss Perspectives

Edited by Courtney J. Fung, Björn Gehrmann, Rachel F. Madenyika, and Jason G. Tower

Routledge
Taylor & Francis Group
LONDON AND NEW YORK

First published 2021
by Routledge
2 Park Square, Milton Park, Abingdon, Oxon OX14 4RN

and by Routledge
605 Third Avenue, New York, NY 10158

Routledge is an imprint of the Taylor & Francis Group, an informa business

© 2021 selection and editorial matter, Courtney J. Fung, Björn Gehrmann, Rachel F. Madenyika, and Jason G. Tower; individual chapters, the contributors

The right of Courtney J. Fung, Björn Gehrmann, Rachel F. Madenyika, and Jason G. Tower to be identified as the authors of the editorial material, and of the authors for their individual chapters, has been asserted in accordance with sections 77 and 78 of the Copyright, Designs and Patents Act 1988.

Trademark notice: Product or corporate names may be trademarks or registered trademarks, and are used only for identification and explanation without intent to infringe.

British Library Cataloguing-in-Publication Data
A catalogue record for this book is available from the British Library

Library of Congress Cataloging-in-Publication Data
Names: Fung, Courtney J., editor.
Title: New paths and policies towards conflict prevention: Chinese and Swiss perspectives / edited by Courtney J. Fung, Björn Gehrmann, Rachel F. Madenyika, and Jason G. Tower.
Description: Abingdon, Oxon ; New York, NY : Routledge, 2021. |
Series: Studies in conflict, development and peacebuilding |
Includes bibliographical references and index.
Identifiers: LCCN 2020049802 (print) | LCCN 2020049803 (ebook) |
ISBN 9780367683368 (hardback) | ISBN 9781003136996 (ebook)
Subjects: LCSH: Pacific settlement of international disputes. |
Peace-building–China. | Peace-building–Switzerland. |
Conflict management–China. | Conflict management–Switzerland |
International cooperation–China. | International cooperation–Switzerland.
Classification: LCC JZ6010 .N48 2021 (print) |
LCC JZ6010 (ebook) | DDC 327.1/72–dc23
LC record available at https://lccn.loc.gov/2020049802
LC ebook record available at https://lccn.loc.gov/2020049803

ISBN: 978-0-367-68336-8 (hbk)
ISBN: 978-0-367-68341-2 (pbk)
ISBN: 978-1-003-13699-6 (ebk)

Typeset in Times New Roman
by Newgen Publishing UK

Contents

Contributors

Courtney J. Fung is Assistant Professor of International Relations at the University of Hong Kong.

Björn Gehrmann is a German Diplomat and Mediator MAS ETH MPP, who worked for the Human Security Division of the Swiss Federal Department of Foreign Affairs from 2017 to 2019.

Yin He is Associate Professor, China Peacekeeping Police Training Center, Langfang.

Stephanie C. Hofmann is Professor of International Relations and Political Science, Graduate Institute of International and Development Studies, Geneva.

David Lanz is currently co-head of the swisspeace Mediation Program and lecturer at the University of Basel.

Dongyan Li is Senior Fellow, Institute of World Economics and Politics, Chinese Academy of Social Sciences, Beijing.

Tiewa Liu is Associate Professor, School of International Relations and Diplomacy, Beijing Foreign Studies University, Beijing.

Rachel F. Madenyika is UN Representative at the Quaker United Nations Office in New York, USA.

Katia Papagianni is Director for Policy and Mediation Support, Centre for Humanitarian Dialogue, Geneva.

Dominic Rohner is Professor of Economics, University of Lausanne, Lausanne.

Albrecht Schnabel is Head of the Asia-Pacific Unit, DCAF – Geneva Centre for Security Sector Governance, Geneva.

Jason G. Tower directs the Burma program of the United States Institute of Peace. (Formerly Southeast Asia Regional Advisor, PeaceNexus Foundation, Yangon).

Guihong Zhang is Director, Centre for UN Studies at the Institute of International Studies, Fudan University, Shanghai.

Acknowledgments

We would like to extend our sincerest gratitude to the scholars whose dedication and selfless commitment of time over a period of two years made this project a success. Deep appreciation goes also to the Swiss Federal Department of Foreign Affairs, which provided generous funding to this endeavor and was substantially involved in the successful implementation of the project. Special thanks go to Björn Gehrmann, Rachel F. Madenyika, and Jason G. Tower, who collaboratively worked to organize the project and were instrumental in facilitating the dialogue, in working with the scholars to support the ideas behind their papers, and in co-editing this volume. Thanks are extended also to the many colleagues who provided comments on the draft versions of this publication, and especial thanks go to Courtney J. Fung (Assistant Professor of International Relations, University of Hong Kong), who worked closely with all the scholars in editing their draft contributions.

The perspectives and conclusion presented in this volume are those of the respective authors and do not necessarily reflect the views of the Quaker United Nations Office, New York, the American Friends Service Committee, PeaceNexus Foundation, or the Swiss Federal Department of Foreign Affairs.

Acronyms

AFSC	American Friends Service Committee
ARF	ASEAN Regional Forum
ASEAN	Association of Southeast Asian Nations
AU	African Union
AUBP	AU Border Programme
BRI	Belt and Road Initiative
BRICS	Brazil, Russia, India, China, and South Africa
CEWS	Continental Early Warning System
CPPTC	China Peacekeeping Police Training Center
DAC	Development Assistance Committee
DCAF	Geneva Centre for Security Sector Governance
DPA	UN Department of Political Affairs
ETA	Euskadi Ta Askatasuna
EU	European Union
FDFA	Swiss Federal Department of Foreign Affairs
FWCC	Friends World Committee for Consultation
GDP	Gross Domestic Product
HPC	High Preparatory Committee
ICRC	International Committee for the Red Cross
IMF	International Monetary Fund
MSU	Mediation Support Unit
NGO	Non-Governmental Organization
OSCE	Organization for Security and Cooperation in Europe
PMD	Policy and Mediation Division
PoW	Panel of the Wise
QUNO	Quaker United Nations Office
SDGs	Sustainable Development Goals
SSG	Security Sector Governance
SSR	Security Sector Reform

TC   Technical Committee
UN   United Nations
UNDP   United Nations Development Programme
UNICEF United Nations Children's Fund
WTO   World Trade Organization

Introduction

Understanding conflict prevention in the shifting global context

Rachel F. Madenyika and Jason G. Tower

The Charter of the United Nations, adopted in the immediate aftermath of the Second World War, is clear about the fundamental necessity for the international community to act in partnership to prevent violent conflict. The Charter is also clear that this must be a multi-dimensional endeavor, which requires that equal weight be given to peace and security, economic and social development, and human dignity.

As the ninth Secretary-General of the United Nations (UN), António Guterres, took office, two trends became apparent. First, the international community increasingly focused on addressing prevention, with a growing realization of the relationships between human displacement, humanitarian need, inequality and exclusion, climate change, and an increase in potential and actual violent conflict. Second, given shifts in global power dynamics, the need was apparent for international policy issues to be addressed in a way that is inclusive of a wider variety of perspectives and approaches.

In particular, it has become clear that Chinese policy actors are increasingly interested in fostering their own discourse on issues of prevention and peacebuilding, rooted in Chinese experience, and engaging with peers from other contexts. China's position has evolved from one of "entering the world" to one of global leadership. In a relatively short time, China has signed agreements and launched initiatives covering a wide range of global governance issues, including monetary policies, currency exchange, trade, anti-corruption, and peace and security (Tower). Compared with China's involvement in global governance just a decade ago, the change is dramatic, and there is therefore a timely opportunity for dialogue with international peers on these central themes.

Against this background, the Quaker United Nation Office (QUNO) and the American Friends Service Committee (AFSC)[1], in collaboration with PeaceNexus and in close partnership with the Swiss Federal Department of Foreign Affairs (FDFA), jointly organized a series of dialogues that took place in Switzerland, China, and the United States. This pilot project sought to intensify the exchange between five Chinese and five Swiss researchers on ways of contributing to the ongoing United Nations' and international debate on peacebuilding in general, and the prevention of violent conflict in particular. The seminars strategically aimed to deepen the mutual understanding of the notion of prevention, and of existing and new instruments available to prevent violent conflicts from emerging, continuing, or relapsing, and to identify areas for cooperation. The researchers explored the rationale for conflict prevention and reviewed prevailing academic and practitioner discourses on fundamental questions, such as why conflicts should be prevented and whether "mainstream approaches" are still relevant. What mechanisms and tools exist to prevent conflict, and how effective is prevention today? What opportunities and challenges exist in preventive diplomacy efforts?

The project was designed to promote trust and relationship-building among the Chinese and Swiss scholars as they shared their insights and experience while exploring common ground. In designing the dialogue sessions, special care was taken to avoid any appearance of a contest or competition between points of view. The premise was that providing a protected space for these discussions would allow a more complete picture of preventive approaches to emerge and encourage forward thinking in this field. During this project, the scholars collaboratively developed a comprehensive list of thematic policy areas that each contributed to this joint publication. Interest in developing future conversations on the topic of mediation was deemed the strongest achievement of this dialogue, especially given that there are so few scholars working on international conflict mediation in China.

The innovations this project represents are important to the discourse on conflict prevention. There have been few dialogues between Chinese and Western scholars on conflict prevention and peacebuilding. Peace and conflict studies as a discipline in China is relatively new, and it is only recently that China started to develop this field. While in some quarters there is a notion that Chinese views are at odds with Western views and vice versa, the project by methodology and design proved otherwise. It promoted trust and relationship-building among the scholars as they shared insights and experience by exploring common ground.

Approaches to the idea of prevention are constantly developing, and the scholars provided considerable richness of perspectives, which fell easily into infinite areas of work. By providing a protected space for these discussions, a more complete picture of preventive approaches emerged, particularly around the peace and development nexus. This project built a space where scholars could engage openly, take risks, and share perspectives on debates within each country. This was achieved by considering different traditions, barriers, blockages, and areas for cooperation. Throughout the project, scholars grappled with some of the key questions in the literature on the effectiveness of peacebuilding, and the role of multilateral organizations in conflict prevention and peacebuilding relevant to sequencing and institutional reform. Scholars further identified how approaches to addressing violent conflict might in some cases be managed, and in other cases be leveraged to build a stronger foundation for cooperation.

Towards a multi-dimensional response to complex crises

In recent years, the repeated occurrence of global peace and security crises has raised significant doubts about the capacity of the United Nations to prevent violence and maintain security. Since 2010, the number of major violent conflicts has tripled, while a growing number of lower intensity conflicts have experienced significant escalation (World Bank and United Nations). A combination of global challenges including climate change, illicit trafficking, and shifting global power structures has contributed to the growing level of crises and has made societies more vulnerable to conflict. Transformations in technology, demographics, labor, and trade have greatly enhanced global awareness of crises, bringing populations closer together and helping to reduce poverty, but have simultaneously brought new challenges that an aging global security architecture struggles to meet successfully (World Bank and United Nations). At the same time, the world's most fragile and marginalized communities enjoy few of the benefits of these changes and bear the greatest shares of the costs of conflict.

Recent research has allowed the international community to begin quantifying the costs of conflict. In 2016, the economic impact of violent conflict resulted in a global economic loss of 30 trillion USD, exceeding global Gross Domestic Product (GDP) by 14.76 trillion USD. In per capita terms, this translates into a loss of nearly 2,000 USD per person (Institute for Economics & Peace). The vast economic losses suffered globally because of conflict represent one of the most compelling arguments for long-term conflict prevention. According to the 2018 Global Peace Index, the average level of global peacefulness has declined for the fourth consecutive year. Thus, the international community can no longer afford to under-invest in prevention and should make it a priority for action.

In 2015, amidst these crises, the UN system came together to achieve landmark outcomes including the 2030 Agenda for Sustainable Development and the Paris Agreement on climate change. Both received universal backing from the UN membership (Boutellis and Ó Súilleabháin). Aspirations to further strengthen the UN's coherence, effectiveness, and ability to respond are evident in the comprehensive examinations of its peace and security efforts. During the same year, three reviews on peacebuilding, peace operations, and the implementation of the women, peace, and security agenda were conducted. The reviews pointed to the urgent need to bring together different parts of the UN system around a long-term vision of peace, one that did not follow the common linear and sequenced approach to conflict response, but was rather a strategic commitment to a "culture of prevention" and to work within a "peace continuum" that encompasses "prevention, conflict resolution, peacekeeping, peacebuilding and long-term development" (Guterres, *Challenges and Opportunities*). A common theme that emerged from the three reviews marked a fundamental shift in the UN's understanding of peacebuilding, from a "post-conflict" exercise towards an emphasis on building peace as an ongoing undertaking. By formulating sustaining peace in the resolutions as "a goal and process … aimed at preventing the outbreak, escalation, continuation and recurrence of conflict" (70/262 and 2282 respectively), the dual resolutions on peacebuilding and sustaining peace adopted unanimously by all nations in the General Assembly and Security Council set out to do just that. As a result, for the first time at the UN, "peacebuilding" and "prevention" have become close to synonymous under this new umbrella term – "Sustaining Peace". Under this new framework, prevention is central, particularly when it is considered as a function of sustainable development and inclusive governance.

The nature of the problem

Under existing dominant paradigms and through its symbiotic relationship to conflict, prevention at the UN continues to be conceived as a nationally owned and driven strategy for averting the outbreak of conflict and sustaining peace. The lack of conceptual clarity regarding the meaning of conflict prevention and what it entails makes it an unwieldly topic for rigorous study. However, some actors are beginning to understand conflict prevention differently, as seen in academia and at the policy level. In the 1990s, students of conflict prevention

such as Munuera and Lund (*Conflict Prevention*) saw conflict prevention as "primarily diplomatic measures and actions used in regions
of high vulnerability to prevent the escalation of tensions into armed
conflict" (Carayannis and Stein). Along the same lines, Secretary-
General Boutros-Ghali's preventive diplomacy understood the concept
as "action taken to prevent disputes from arising between parties, and
to prevent existing disputes from escalating into conflicts" (Boutros-
Ghali). On the other hand, authors such as Wallensteen referred to prevention as actions that can prevent conflict, without limiting the tools to
diplomatic means. More recently, a UN–World Bank report questioned
the long-standing assumption that income growth alone leads to peace,
and introduced the business case for prevention: "the expected returns
on prevention will be positive so long as the costs of prevention are
less than the damages and/or losses due to violence" (World Bank and
United Nations).

While the term "prevention" seems to be accepted at the policy
level, neither policymakers nor scholars agree on timing, sequencing,
or required necessary tools. The dichotomy of prevention is evident,
as operational prevention – "pre-empting the eruption of violence"
(Lund, "Preventing Violent Intrastate Conflicts") – and long-term
structural prevention efforts that tackle root causes of conflict are
both necessary. First introduced in the final report of the Carnegie
Commission launched in 1997, both operational and structural prevention are considered equally important approaches that may be applied
dependent on the stage of a particular conflict. At one end of the spectrum are the operational preventive activities which rely on third-party
interventions for the prevention of imminent conflict or escalation.
On the other end of the spectrum are activities which focus on the
deep-rooted causes of conflict and "aim to strengthen the institutions
and social mechanisms of states and societies, helping them to become
more resilient to the causes and triggers of conflict" (United Nations,
Conflict Prevention). In the 2001 Report of the Secretary-General on
Prevention of Armed Conflict, "an effective preventive strategy" is said
to require "a comprehensive approach that encompasses both short-
term and long-term political, diplomatic, humanitarian, human rights,
developmental, institutional, and other measures taken by the international community, in cooperation with national and regional actors"
(United Nations, *Prevention of Armed Conflict*). Consensus on the
scope of conflict prevention is essential as conceptual parameters are
critical for establishing and maintaining effective conflict prevention
strategies.

Emerging ideas for peace

Two streams of literature have developed relevant to academic discourse on prevention in China. The first is at the nexus of Chinese foreign policy and security studies, and the second at the nexus of peace and development. While still nascent, these literatures in their own right are in dialogue with both Western, and in some cases, other global discourses on these issues. That said, as might be expected, they are also deeply rooted in China's own political traditions and influenced by pragmatic needs around China's rapidly shifting international role.

When considering Chinese foreign policy and security studies, Chinese scholars seek to explore challenges emerging around China's traditional foreign policy principles of peaceful coexistence, non-intervention in domestic affairs of states, and new needs relevant to involvement in security governance (Wang, *Creative Involvement*). Current debates center around the primacy of the state versus non-state actors in addressing security challenges; how to address Western and especially American dominance of international institutions; how to draw lessons from ancient Chinese models of global governance that might be applicable to the modern day (Yan); and how to address issues of growing institutional competition as China develops a role as a provider of global governance goods.

In the second area of debate on the peace and development nexus, the key focus centers on China's experiences over 40 years of reform, which have prioritized economic development as a means of maintaining and enhancing stability (Wang and Hu). Some Chinese scholars argue that Western approaches focus too much on resolving governance issues, and not enough on addressing development in the form of infrastructure, job creation, and market development (He). In some cases, scholars have argued for a "developmental peace" as a counter to "liberal peace". Critics of this perspective point out that not all forms of development will lead to peace and focus on some of the lessons that China has learned over the past decade in promoting large-scale development when it comes to promoting peace projects. Examples from Myanmar – where China supported large-scale dams adjacent to ceasefire lines – have drawn considerable attention from Chinese scholars arguing for a more nuanced view of the relationship between development and peace (Jiang).

So, how can the global community more effectively prevent violent conflict, as violent conflicts have become more complex and protracted? While acknowledging the challenges of definition, timing, sequencing, and choice of tools, proving when prevention works remains a significant hurdle. It is therefore imperative to understand the normative and political impact of sustaining peace in diverse contexts.

To contribute towards strengthening such understanding, this book identifies tools that help navigate today's uncertainties and attempts to conceptualize tomorrow's practice of international peacebuilding and conflict prevention. The volume seeks to answer questions such as: Why should conflicts be prevented? Are "mainstream approaches" are still relevant? What mechanisms and tools exist to prevent conflict; how effective is prevention today? And, what opportunities and challenges exist in preventive diplomacy efforts?

The book makes the case for conflict prevention and provides insights for practitioners of peacebuilding and international relations such as policymakers, philanthropists, diplomats, development workers, researchers, and students.

Part I: the broader norms of prevention and building peace

The first section of this volume addresses prevention and resolution of violent conflict from a macro-political as well as micro-economic perspective. It asks three fundamental questions: (1) How do we sustain peace? (2) Why should we promote peace and prevent war? (3) How should we actually go about doing it? In his contribution, Björn Gehrmann offers a consideration of the shortcomings of various approaches to international peacebuilding. He identifies three practical measures which function to sustain peace by eliminating the drivers of conflict: investments in economic development; alignment of political institutions; and how information is shared between conflicting parties. His chapter "How to sustain peace: a review of the scholarly debate" embraces the importance of these three measures as central to sustaining peace and suggests that the UN enhance its investment in research on the causes of war. In the following chapter, "Political violence prevention: definitions and implications", Stephanie C. Hofmann stresses that conflict prevention policies already exist in the peace and development nexus. She underscores that the reinvigoration of concepts alone is not enough to create a policy but that normative concepts, mechanisms, resources, and capacities need to be attached to such concepts. She provides an overview of these concepts in various contexts including the United Nations, World Bank, European Union, and African Union. Yin He, in the next chapter "A tale of two 'peaces': peacebuilding in the twenty-first century: liberal peace, developmental peace, and peacebuilding" stresses that liberal peace overemphasizes institution building, and places too little emphasis on development. In his view, developmental peace more effectively helps address the economic drivers of conflict than efforts to build institutions. He further highlights that their coexistence can greatly benefit the peacebuilding of post-conflict states and explores means for building better coordination mechanisms between the two types of approaches. In the subsequent chapter, "How to curb conflict: policy lessons from the economic literature", Dominic Rohner looks at peacebuilding through an economic lens. He concludes that while the literature in conflict economics has gained an overview on major causes and consequences of armed fighting, up until recently the study of how particular policies can reduce conflict risks has been neglected. He recommends further empirical policy research in this area. In his view, it is especially important to look at how different types of development interventions and different forms of economic support impact armed conflict.

Part II: approaches to preventing conflict

Part II of this volume presents elements of the approaches to peacebuilding. David Lanz's chapter on "The deep roots of Swiss conflict prevention" draws attention to how conflict prevention represents a fundamental interest for Switzerland, given its disposition as a small state with a federal structure and a heterogeneous society. Lanz argues that, therefore, conflict prevention does not automatically emerge, but is outcome of accommodation and negotiations between different groups within the country. The Swiss culture of conflict management thus differs fundamentally from the Chinese approach even if the two countries share a similar interest in the reduction of political violence. In her practice-oriented chapter, "Considerations for the design and preparation of national dialogue processes", Katia Papagianni discusses the utility of national dialogues, a peace strategy that is used in conflict situations where political power within a country is widely dispersed among various groups, and where a new coalition government needs to be created. The chapter explains how national dialogue processes need to tackle the difficult decisions on what needs to be discussed and resolved, identifying key participants, designing the dialogue format, and above all being flexible and creative throughout the process. In the following chapter, "China and mediation: principles and practice", Tiewa Liu maintains that China's fundamental principles of non-intervention and non-use of force remain intact, but that China is currently working on integrating facilitative, evaluative, and transformative mediation approaches into its foreign policy. Mediation can be a successful tool in achieving stability in volatile contexts where China has investments, and it can contribute to China's long-run national interests and international responsibilities.

Part III: opportunities for peace

In Part III, elements of the developmental approach to peace promotion are addressed. In her chapter titled "How to understand the peacebuilding potential of the Belt and Road Initiative", Dongyan Li points out that the peacebuilding potential of the Belt and Road Initiative has not been fully leveraged by BRI partners, and that this is a critical growth area. From a UN peacebuilding perspective, and as BRI is an economic cooperation–led initiative, China can and should make a strong contribution to UN peacebuilding and conflict prevention. Albrecht Schnabel's contribution "Security sector reform and conflict prevention" sums up that security sector reform (SSR) is vital for conflict prevention and is key for successful regional cooperation, business, and development. He puts emphasis on linking the Swiss interest in providing SSR support with Chinese interests in advancing peace through development of an effective state, including a strong security sector, as part of the Belt and Road Initiative. Guihong Zhang outlines that the main goal and design of Chinese major power diplomacy in the new era is the idea of a "community of shared future for mankind", as proposed by President Xi Jinping. In his contribution to this volume, "'A community of shared future for mankind' and implications for conflict prevention", Zhang states that this idea will undoubtedly have implications for world peace and security and needs to be integrated with existing international principles and norms or transformed into new ones.

In the concluding chapter, "Future collaborative efforts to prevent conflict", Rachel F. Madenyika and Jason G. Tower draw together the main themes and purpose of the project and volume and present: (1) the importance and impact of dialogue for prevention; and (2) the need to explore instruments and tools that are compatible with peace narratives, such as mediation, providing an opportunity for collaboration and an appetite to learn, diversify, and understand approaches to peace.

About the organizations

Quaker United Nations Office, New York (QUNO)

Since 1947, QUNO, supported by the American Friends Service Committee (AFSC) and the Friends World Committee for Consultation

(FWCC), has worked with diplomats, UN officials, and civil society to support a UN that prioritizes peace and prevents war. Grounded in the Quaker belief that there is that of the divine in every person, we seek a United Nations that addresses key drivers of violence including structures and systems that produce exclusion and injustice; that facilitates and supports change through peaceful means; and whose policies and practices reflect a diversity of voices, such that people around the world can safely and peacefully achieve their potential. QUNO uses Quaker House and its convening power to facilitate off-the-record meetings and bring perspectives from outside the UN system in order to promote peacebuilding and the prevention of violent conflict at a policy level in New York.

American Friends Service Committee (AFSC)

Founded in 1917, the American Friends Service Committee is a Quaker organization that promotes lasting peace with justice, as a practical expression of faith in action.

PeaceNexus Foundation

PeaceNexus is a Switzerland-based foundation established in May 2009. The PeaceNexus core mission is to provide peacebuilding-relevant actors – multilateral organizations, governments, non-profit organizations, and business actors – with expertise and advice on how they can make best use of their peacebuilding role and capacity to help stabilize and reconcile conflict-affected societies. PeaceNexus specializes in identifying relevant and cutting-edge expertise, making it available to actors for peacebuilding, and structuring, sequencing, and accompanying the advisory process. It played a key role in facilitating both the fourth round of dialogue in this project and the launch event for the publication.

Swiss Federal Department of Foreign Affairs

The Human Security Division of the Swiss Federal Department of Foreign Affairs is responsible for the promotion of peace, human rights, and democracy. In the area of peace policy, it focuses on the prevention and resolution of violent conflict and efforts to ensure lasting peace.

Note

1 Since 2009, QUNO and AFSC have engaged leading global Chinese academics on issues related to coordinated approaches to peacebuilding and the prevention of violent conflict through multilateral platforms. Identifying that Chinese researchers had limited field-level engagement with a spectrum of peace operations, and especially with early warning, peacebuilding, and mediation, QUNO and AFSC worked to support Chinese academics' engagement and fieldwork, looking at the involvement of China and other key donor states in this space. This effort was catalytic, with Chinese participants publishing a wide range of policy and academic papers on a broad spectrum of peace operations and peacebuilding.

Bibliography

Aggestam, K. "Conflict Prevention: Old Wine in New Bottles?" *International Peacekeeping*, vol. 10, no. 1, 2003.

Boutellis, Arthur, and Andrea Ó Súilleabháin. *Working Together for Peace: Synergies and Connectors for Implementing the 2015 UN Reviews*. New York, International Peace Institute, May 2016.

Boutros-Ghali, Boutros. *An Agenda for Peace: Preventive Diplomacy, Peacemaking and Peace-Keeping*. United Nations, 1992.

Carayannis, Tatiana, and Sabrina Stein. "Prevention: The Challenge of Theory and Practice". *Humanitarianism: A Dictionary of Concepts*, edited by Tim Allen et al., New York, Routledge, 2018.

Guterres, António. "Challenges and Opportunities for the United Nations". HuffPost, 5 Nov. 2016.

Guterres, António. "A UN of the Future to Effectively Serve All Member States". Letter from the Secretary-General to United Nations Member States, 31 May, 2017.

He, Yin. "Development Peace: The Chinese Approach to United Nations Peacekeeping and Peacebuilding". *International Political Research*, vol. 4, 2017.

Institute for Economics & Peace. *Global Peace Index 2018: Measuring Peace in a Complex World*. Sydney, June 2018, www.economicsandpeace.org/wp-content/uploads/2020/08/Global-Peace-Index-2018-2-1.pdf.

Jiang, Heng. *Out of the Mine Fields and Blind Areas of Overseas Investment Security*. Beijing, China Economic Publishing House, 2014.

Lund, Michael. *Conflict Prevention: Theory in Pursuit of Policy and Practice*. 1996.

Lund, Michael. "Preventing Violent Intrastate Conflicts: Learning lessons from Experience". *Searching for Peace in Europe and Eurasia: An Overview of Conflict Prevention and Peacebuilding Activities*, edited by Paul van Tongeren et al., London, Lynne Rienner Publishers, Inc., 2002.

Munuera, Gabriel. *Preventing Armed Conflict in Europe: Lessons from Recent Experience*. Paris, France, Institute for Security Studies, 1994.

Tower, Jason G. *Conflict Dynamics and the Belt and Road Initiative: Ignoring Conflict on the "Road to Peace".* Berlin, Bread of the World Foundation, 2020, www.brot-fuer-die-welt.de/fileadmin/mediapool/downloads/fach publikationen/analyse/Analyse97-en.pdf.

United Nations. "An Agenda for Peace: Preventive Diplomacy and Related Matters". 1992.

————. General Assembly Resolution 60/1 (24 Oct. 2005), 2005 World Summit Outcome. UN Doc. A/RES/60/1, para. 74.

————. *Prevention of Armed Conflict: Report of the Secretary-General* [A/55/985–S/2001/574], 2001.

————. *United Nations Conflict Prevention and Preventive Diplomacy in Action: An Overview of the Role, Approach and Tools of the United Nations and its Partners in Preventing Violent Conflict.* United Nations, 2017.

Wallensteen, Peter. "Preventive Security: Direct and Structural Prevention of Violent Conflicts". *Preventing Violent Conflict: Past Record and Future Challenges*, edited by Peter Wallensteen, Uppsala, Sweden, Uppsala University, Department of Peace and Conflict Research, 1998.

Wallensteen, P., and Möller, F. "Conflict Prevention: Methodology for Knowing the Unknown" *Uppsala Peace Research Papers*, no. 7, Department of Peace and Conflict Research, Uppsala University, 2003.

Wang, Lei, and Hu, Angang, "Empirical Research on the Relationship between Economic Development and Socio-Political Stability: A Comparative Analysis Based on Multi-National Data". *Comparative Social and Economic Institutions*, vol. 1, 2010, pp. 83–89.

Wang, Yizhou. *Creative Involvement: A New Direction in China's Diplomacy.* Beijing, Beijing UP, 2011.

World Bank and United Nations. *Pathways for Peace: Inclusive Approaches to Preventing Violent Conflict.* World Bank and UN, 2018, doi:10.1596/978-1-4648-1162-3.

Yan, Xuetong. *Ancient Chinese Thought, Modern Chinese Power.* Princeton, Princeton UP, 2011.

Part I

The broader norms of prevention and building peace

1 How to sustain peace

A review of the scholarly debate

Björn Gehrmann[1]

Sustaining Peace: a new paradigm for international peacebuilding?

International peacebuilding is in a state of transition. This is probably best exemplified by the comprehensive reorganization of the United Nations' political–operational structure, which was commissioned by UN member states as part of the "Sustaining Peace" resolutions of both Security Council and General Assembly, and executed by the UN's new Secretary-General, António Guterres, shortly after he took office in 2017 (United Nations *Peacebuilding and Sustaining Peace*). This transition was triggered by two expert reports on the state of peacebuilding at the United Nations. In 2015, UN member states commissioned reviews of the existing approach to peace operations (by establishing a High-Level Independent Panel on United Nations Peace Operations) and the international peacebuilding architecture (by way of an "Advisory Group of Experts for the 2015 Review of the United Nations Peacebuilding Architecture"). Both reviews eschewed the language of peacebuilding in favor of "Sustaining Peace" (United Nations *Challenge of Sustaining Peace, Uniting Our Strengths*). The reports caused the international community to reconsider its approach to peace operations and peacebuilding. Referring to the insights of these reports, the Security Council and the General Assembly of the United Nations passed twin resolutions on "Sustaining Peace", which embody this policy shift within the UN. The resolutions aim at strengthening the nexus between peace and security, sustainable development, and human rights. The main objective of the "Sustaining Peace" agenda is to establish a "holistic approach" that results in a more coherent UN policy and strengthens mutually reinforcing linkages between the UN's three pillars. In accordance with the Sustaining Peace approach, UN Secretary-General Guterres newly emphasizes the UN's role in the prevention of political violence, which is based on the "recognition that efforts to sustain peace were necessary not only once conflict had broken out, but also long beforehand, through the prevention of conflict and addressing its root causes" (United Nations *Peacebuilding and Sustaining Peace*).

One of the most striking characteristics of the Sustaining Peace agenda is its emphasis on conflict prevention. In her chapter for this book, Stephanie Hofmann points out that conflict prevention should not be a goal in itself, since conflict as such is neither good nor bad. Instead, we should primarily be concerned about political violence. However, even a focus on the prevention of political violence does not significantly narrow down available political options. A wide array of policies can still be justified on this basis, along the temporal dimension (prevention of occurrence versus prevention of recurrence) or the instrumental dimension (persuasion versus coercion), as well as in terms of legitimacy (passive prevention versus active prevention) and feasibility (willingness to fight versus ability to fight). In theory, prevention can comprise civilian measures such as strengthening political inclusion of underrepresented groups, and the use of force, especially military interventions. As Hofmann points out, in practice, many international actors engage in prevention, with substantial diversity in terms of the concrete policies pursued.

As David Lanz outlines in this volume, in Switzerland prevention is understood as a purely civilian effort to prevent the occurrence of political violence by addressing a group's willingness to fight, i.e. the root causes of group grievances. Among the instruments utilized are referenda. In contrast, as Guihong Zhang explains, China views its efforts to establish a "new type of international relations" (combining democratization of the international system and rule of law as means to oppose power politics and hegemony) as an effort in the prevention of conflict between states as well as the prevention of military intervention. At the same time, it emphasizes inclusive and sustainable development as the most appropriate tool for the prevention of intra-state conflict.

The scholarly debate about peacebuilding

Deficiencies of the mainstream approach to peacebuilding

On the one hand, observers have increasingly perceived the mainstream approach to peacebuilding, largely inspired by the "Liberal Peace" hypothesis, as deficient. As de Coning ("From Peacebuilding" 166) points out, the belief in the transformative power of international peacebuilding has waned because many of the interventions undertaken …, and especially those in the Balkans, Iraq, Afghanistan and in Africa's Great Lakes, and Horn regions are widely understood to have been ineffective.

The 2015 review of the UN's approach to peacebuilding was preceded by a large number of critical assessments of peacebuilding by scholars (for a comprehensive overview of the critical debate on peacebuilding see Chetail and Jütersonke). The academic critique usually subsumes some themes of the UN peacebuilding into the broader liberal peacebuilding agenda, which emerged from an optimistic interpretation of preliminary empirical results from studies of inter-state warfare. Since liberal democracies almost never go to war, many scholars and politicians expected that a transition from authoritarian rule to democratic governance within states would bring peace (Doyle "Liberalism"; Maoz and Russett; Owen). On the basis of these findings, US president Bill Clinton presented in his 1994 State of the Union speech a new foreign policy agenda, the central aim of which was to promote democratization around the globe. The grand ambition was to establish a Liberal Peace, based on three pillars: republican representation, commitment to fundamental human rights, and transnational interdependence (Doyle "Three Pillars").[2] Liberal Peace became the dominant narrative of post–Cold War foreign affairs and served as inspiration for diverse foreign policy initiatives such as the foundation of the World Trade Organization, NATO and EU enlargement, robust UN peace operations (based on the "responsibility to protect"), and military interventions in countries such as Iraq and Afghanistan.

However, since its first formulation in the 1980s, the Liberal Peace hypothesis has been subject to critical scholarly scrutiny. The critique consists of two parts. The first strand of criticism addresses the concept of liberal peacebuilding as such. In an influential piece, Mansfield and Snyder ("Democratization") criticize the proponents' "naive enthusiasm" and argue for a strategy of "limited goals", contending that rapidly democratizing states are disproportionately likely to fight wars. Empirical scholars point out that Liberal Peace is a normative concept, a hypothesis that has been tested over and over, but whose causality has never been entirely confirmed (Hegre). The second strand of criticism mainly refers to the flawed implementation of a sound approach to peacebuilding by an irrationally exuberant international community. Observers have compared the "irrational exuberance" of liberal peacebuilders with the mistaken beliefs of the apostles of efficient markets (Paris). Economists are often credited (or blamed) for coming up with the famous "efficient markets hypothesis", which was used to justify a policy advocating for a more prominent role of the financial sector in society. However, the Global Financial Crisis is a manifest example of the shortcomings of this policy, which subsequently became an issue of national significance in the United States, culminating in a Congressional Hearing examining the flaws of the underlying economic ideas and concepts.[3] The second strand of critique states that "the challenge today is not to replace or move 'beyond' liberal peacebuilding, but to reform existing approaches within a broadly liberal framework" (Paris 362).

Regardless of these critiques, Liberal Peace remains the fallback peace narrative, reflected in the foreign policies of the international community and the countries of the Western hemisphere. It remains to be seen to which degree the UN's Sustaining Peace approach will be able to modify the liberal approach to peacebuilding. Critical observers have already pointed to the fact that Sustaining Peace in its current, embryonic form is "not specific enough to be operationalized" (de Coning "Sustaining Peace").

Emerging designs for peace

In a parallel development that is independent of the peacebuilding community's internal reflections, new ideas for peace are emerging in the wake of a global wealth shift. This shift is mostly due to the impact of globalization, itself a product of the post-1989 liberal drive towards transnational interdependence, on economic growth in Asia. Growth is shifting from "the West" to "the East", mainly China. One of the consequences of this process of economic catch-up is an "Easternization" of global politics (Rachman). As part of this process, emerging countries, first and foremost China, have increased their financial support for international institutions. At the UN, this has manifested itself – among other things – in a significant increase in Chinese support for UN peacekeeping operations (Stahle). At the same time, however, non-Western support for the United Nations' peacebuilding efforts in conflict-afflicted and post-conflict states has not picked up in the same fashion. For mostly political reasons, China has pursued a strategy of "selectively cautious participation" in UN peacebuilding operations (L. Zhao 354). As Zhao (351) describes, China – while it has shown flexibility in practice – "is not in favor of peacebuilding conflated with military action, humanitarian intervention or regime change, and vigorously opposes any state-building operations". It is only recently that Chinese scholars have become more vocal in proposing alternative ways to achieve "positive peace". Based on the assumption that "a country's international peace intervention policy is a ... projection of a domestic peace experience onto foreign countries" (Wang 71), China is pioneering an approach that combines promoting peace and stability through social and economic development. The new term being coined for the Chinese approach to peacebuilding is "developmental peace" (Wang). It emphasizes the idea that "security and development are intrinsically linked, and peacebuilding would be impossible without achievement on the development front" (L. Zhao 352).

The Chinese approach is informed by more than a decade of first-hand experience in developing countries, mainly in Sub-Saharan Africa. It rests on two central pillars: sovereignty (implying political non-interference from the outside), and non-politicized development. They translate into two essential peace strategies: (1) promotion of economic and social development in terms of GDP per capita, in the absence of demands for enhanced financial governance;[4] and (2) prioritization of the role of the state, backing state development initiatives where they may be found, with minimal reference to public perceptions or opposition voices to such initiatives.[5] Notably, this approach does not prominently feature a normative political ambition in terms of promoting liberalization of the existing type of political regime. As such, the role of civil society is not emphasized, and there is no essential focus on public participation and/or strengthening of accountability of government (Wang).

Empirical reality check: which measures sustain peace?

The debate about the best approach to sustaining peace is primarily political. However, in parallel to the political debate, a young but growing scientific literature has started to produce important insights about the conditions for achieving and sustaining peace. In his chapter for this volume, Dominic Rohner introduces four generic policies for peace: (1) stability, (2) incentives, (3) institutions, and (4) trust. All four options are a product of empirical research into the causes of war. Each deals with a different cause. Whereas the first approach (stability) deals only with an opposition's *ability to fight*, the latter three deal with its *willingness to fight*, i.e. with the root causes of conflict.

The reason for investments in stability – nowadays commonly referred to as *stabilization* – is weakness of the government, especially in security terms. The underlying logic is simple: in a political contest, the party with better military capabilities usually secures victory. Therefore, investments in the capacity of the government, first and foremost into its enforcement (or repressive) capacity, should be able to deter potential insurgents from taking up arms against the government. Measures include capacity building for military, police, and judiciary through financing, equipment, training, and advice. Stabilization does not address root causes of conflict such as individual poverty or group grievances. It prevents political violence through deterrence or ends it through repression, resulting in a state of "negative peace". As Albrecht Schnabel explains in his essay for this volume, enforcement capacity can be achieved through security sector reform, especially by establishing an uncontested monopoly of violence. In other words, the state disables the opposition's ability to fight; however, it does not target its willingness to fight. The problem with this approach is that in case of a military windfall for the opposition (e.g. through wealthy outside sponsors), war would still occur (due to the opposition's continued willingness to fight).[6] Some observers criticize that stabilization represents an overly transactional approach to conflict resolution, neglecting the root causes of the conflict. They fear that it is becoming the preferred intervention type of the countries of the Western hemisphere, and that it has, in conjunction with counterterrorism, the potential to at least partially replace Liberal Peace as the dominant peace paradigm (Karlsrud).

The three other strategies are more ambitious. They try to achieve and sustain peace through an elimination of the reasons for engaging in political violence. They will be analyzed in the following subsections.

Peace and institutions

The objective of the first approach is to promote institutions that reduce political violence. This approach goes beyond simple democracy promotion in that it distinguishes between the impacts on peace of different forms of democracies. The basic intuition is that power-sharing mechanisms (such as grand coalitions, proportional representation, not majoritarian representation) and power-dividing mechanisms (vertical separation of powers such as federalism) prevent political groups from using violence to further their goals. In the former case, they do this through the requirement to find a compromise via intra-governmental negotiation, and in the latter case, thanks to the elimination of the requirement to negotiate with rivalling groups (due to the division).

However, Mansfield and Snyder ("Prone to Violence" 42) provide an example that cautions against a one-size-fits-all institutional approach to peace, with a particular concern for the Middle East:

In the Arab world, every state has at least one risk factor for failed, violent democratization. ... Per capita incomes, literacy rates and citizen skills in most Muslim Middle Eastern states are below the levels normally needed to sustain democracy.

If practiced, democracy promotion strategies should be sequenced to try to prevent negative outcomes. In the same spirit, Collier and Rohner (533) propose that in "low-income countries, international promotion of democracy needs to be complemented by international strengthening of security".

Peace and investment

The second approach tackles an individual's incentives to participate in political violence. The underlying idea is to raise her opportunity costs of appropriation (of goods produced by others). This can be achieved either through an increase in the gains from production, i.e. her potential salary in the local labor market, or through a reduction of the gains from engaging in appropriation (political violence, but also economic violence). The former could be achieved through investments in local labor markets (increasing labor demand through employment programs and/or increasing job market access through schooling), the latter through a penalization of forcefully appropriated lootable goods in the respective domestic and international markets (e.g. international certification schemes for "blood diamonds"). As Dominic Rohner points out in his essay, considering available causal evidence, investment in schooling is one of the most promising development-for-peace measures. This approach resembles the Chinese approach of peace through development. It differs, however, in its emphasis on building inalienable capacities of individuals, as opposed to building state capacity, which is, to some extent, alienable. In his essay in this volume, Guihong Zhang describes how there is not one single measure that causes development. In theory, there is a multitude of individual development policies, with different and at times opposing effects on peace – think of uneven economic development between different ethnic groups in the same country, which is viewed as a key risk factor for political violence (Ray and Esteban).

Even though some development measures have been tied to a positive impact in terms of peace, it has not yet been established that investments in infrastructure such as roads, bridges, and hospitals have a direct positive effect on peace. In terms of causality, the best available evidence on Chinese development aid hints to a positive causal effect on growth (Dreher et al.). Recent research also suggests that Chinese development aid, when compared with World Bank development projects, tends to result (a) in more stability when considering less-lethal conflicts by governments against civilians, and (b) in a stronger emphasis on rule-following behavior and a higher acceptance of autocratic regimes (Gehring et al.). As Dongyan Li explains in her essay in this volume, there is reason to believe that the Belt and Road Initiative, with its investments in conflict-affected regions that would otherwise not take place, may offer an interesting potential for peace. However, the Chinese policy of debt-financing infrastructure investments linked to the BRI has elicited the so-called debt trap critique: If BRI "follows Chinese practices to date for infrastructure financing, which often entail lending to sovereign borrowers, then BRI raises the risk of debt distress in some borrower countries" (Hurley et al.). This claim is disputed, however (M. Zhao).

Peace and information

The third approach relies on information and communication, with the aim of establishing inter-group trust. The basic idea is to create mutual benefits, for example through the establishment of economically beneficial trade relations (establishment of inter-group trade associations), or through the re-establishment of psychologically beneficial relations between formerly warring parties (bilateral pacification through, for example, mediation or (national) dialogue), or between perpetrators and victims through the joint treatment of grievances (community reconciliation procedures).

Any successful peace strategy should consider the employment of "open-ended" peace "mechanisms" such as mediation or national dialogue – "open-ended" since they do not contain a prescription for a certain peace policy; "mechanism" since they do not require large capital investments, but rather rely on the willingness of the warring parties to come to a peaceful agreement, coupled with a structured communication process. In many cases, mediation and national dialogues result in a power-sharing arrangement. The main difference between the two mechanisms is the context. Mediation usually occurs in a situation where two parties contest control of government (power duopoly). In her contribution to this volume, Katia Papagianni explains that national dialogues usually occur in situations where a larger number of parties are contesting political control, without a clear incumbent (power oligopoly). Due to their open-endedness, both mechanisms are versatile and compatible with different peace narratives.

As Tiewa Liu points out in her essay for this volume, China has a long-standing mediation culture, which is informed by Confucianism's deeply embedded humanistic values of social harmony, respect for authority, and humility. They manifest in concepts of relationships and "harmony and cooperation". Recent years have seen substantial progress in China's international mediation activities. In countries such as Israel, Afghanistan, Bangladesh, and Syria, among others, diplomats from China increasingly engage in preventing, managing, or resolving conflict. In 2017, mainly triggered by the Belt and Road Initiative, Beijing was involved in nine conflicts (Legarda).

Tailor-made pathways to peace: institutions, investment, and information

Measured against the growing body of the scientific literature, none of the older and newer approaches to peacebuilding unites all of these policies under one umbrella. However, as Yin He demonstrates in his chapter for this book, the successful interplay of different approaches to peace is possible, even desirable. In East Timor, political stability was achieved by way of consensual democracy, and paved the way for a strong government with a priority to invest in development. This case might serve as an inspiration for sustaining peace.

The above example also gives an idea of what an evidence-based approach to peace could look like: thorough diagnosis of the underlying problems, careful choice of appropriate remedies, sequential implementation. The World Bank and the United Nations refer to this approach as the identification of "country pathways to peace", where each country pathway is shaped by "the endogenous risk factors that engender violence and support for countries to address their own crises" (World Bank and United Nations 262).

This review shows that in most contexts, an excessive focus on political institutions or on economic incentives will not be sufficient to achieve peace. This reasoning resonates well with the findings of the *Pathways for Peace* report, which recognizes that "successful conflict prevention strategies increasingly need to align security, development, and diplomatic action over the long term" (World Bank and United Nations). Based on these reflections, how should we go about sustaining peace? As the contributions in this volume show, three general practical measures stand out: (a) *investments* in economic development in conflict-affected regions, (b) efforts to align political *institutions* with the needs of the people, and (c) the transmission of *information* between conflict parties. Sustaining peace could combine the power of the three

Is – Institutions, Investment, and Information – and embrace the hitherto untapped potentials to which recent empirical research points. This could be the beginning of truly complementary policies for peace. That being said, how can we move ahead on this path? In the initially mentioned congressional hearing on the shortcomings of economic theory, the witnesses, were asked: "If economics cannot currently identify emerging conditions that could threaten the Nation's economic wellbeing, what kind of work do we need to fund to receive such insights?" (*Building a Science of Economics*). In a similar vein, we should ask ourselves: "If political scientists and political economists cannot sufficiently identify emerging conditions that threaten a particular country's – or even the world's – peace, what kind of work should the international community fund to receive such insights?" Here is one obvious answer: We need more investment in theoretical and empirical research into the causes and consequences of, and the respective remedies for, war. This echoes the findings of a recent examination of the state of evidence for peace, which diagnoses a "dearth of studies that attempt to measure … actual peace and violence outcomes" (Brown et al. 55). The United Nations, with its mandate for "peace and security", should lead this effort. An important step towards this goal would be to equip the UN with capacities for research that can match those of the World Bank and the International Monetary Fund.

Notes

1 Björn Gehrmann is a German Diplomat and Mediator MAS ETH MPP ("Master of Advanced Studies ETH Mediation in Peace Processes") who worked for the Human Security Division of the Swiss Federal Department of Foreign Affairs from 2017 to 2019. The views expressed in this article are his own and do not necessarily reflect those of the Swiss Federal Department of Foreign Affairs or those of the German Federal Foreign Office.
2 The Liberal Peace relies on a number of smaller political and economic interventions: (1) promotion of republican representation through a strengthening of democratic, participatory norms or through external incentives such as development aid conditioned on compliance with criteria of good governance; (2) promotion of fundamental human rights through international standard setting, either in coded international public law, through the building of global institutions such as the UN Human Rights Council, or through development aid conditioned on compliance with human rights; (3) promotion of cross-border trade and investment through the liberalization of trade and investment by way of multilateral trade agreements and the building of global institutions such as WTO, or through IMF lending

conditioned on compliance with free market standards as embodied in the "Washington Consensus".

3 In the aftermath of the crisis, the (macro-)economics profession was identified as one of the culprits and came under substantial public scrutiny. The Hearing took place in 2010 and was emblematically titled "Building a Science of Economics for the Real World" (*Building a Science of Economics*). Triggered by this unprecedented level of inquiry, macroeconomists started a process of professional introspection, debating the scientific shortcomings of their models and their policy advice, as is evident in a number of recent scientific efforts, such as the "Rebuilding Macroeconomic Theory Project" (Vines and Wills).

4 Mainly through unconditional development aid for infrastructure such as roads, bridges, and hospitals, and loans and investment secured by natural resources or other available equity.

5 For this reason, some scholars refer to it as a "strong state–weak society" model, with a focus on national unity and territorial integrity.

6 Connected to the idea of stability and a strong government are investments in legal capacity (mainly for the protection of property rights) and fiscal capacity (mainly for the collection of taxes); see (Besley and Persson).

Bibliography

Besley, T., and T. Persson. *Pillars of Prosperity: The Political Economics of Development Clusters*. Princeton UP, 2011.

Brown, A. N., F. McCollister, D. B. Cameron, and J. Ludwig. "The Current State of Peacebuilding Programming and Evidence". 3ie Scoping Papers, no. 2, 3ie, 2015.

Building a Science of Economics for the Real World. House of Representatives, 111th Congress, Second Session, 20 July 2010.

Chetail, V., and O. Jütersonke. *Peacebuilding: Critical Concepts in Political Science*. Routledge, 2014.

Collier, P., and D. Rohner. "Democracy, Development, and Conflict". *Journal of the European Economic Association*, vol. 6, no. 2–3, 2008, pp. 531–540, doi:10.1162/jeea.2008.6.2-3.531.

de Coning, C. "From Peacebuilding to Sustaining Peace: Implications of Complexity for Resilience and Sustainability". *Resilience-International Policies Practices and Discourses*, vol. 4, no. 3, 2016, pp. 166–181, doi:10.1080/21693293.2016.1153773.

———. "Sustaining Peace: Can a New Approach Change the UN?" *Global Governance Spotlight*, vol. 3, 2018.

Doyle, M. W. "Liberalism and World Politics". *American Political Science Review*, vol. 80, no. 4, 1986, pp. 1151–1169.

———. "Three Pillars of the Liberal Peace". *American Political Science Review*, vol. 99, no. 3, 2005, pp. 463–466.

Dreher, A., et al. "Aid, China, and Growth: Evidence from a New Global Development Finance Dataset". *AidData Working Papers*, no. 46, AidData, 2017.

Gehring, K., L. C. Kaplan, and M. H. Wong. "Aid and Conflict at the Subnational Level: Evidence from World Bank and Chinese Development Projects in Africa". *AidData Working Papers*, no. 70, AidData, 2019.

Hegre, H. "Democracy and Armed Conflict". *Journal of Peace Research*, vol. 51, no. 2, 2014, pp. 159–172, doi:10.1177/0022343313512852.

Hurley, J., S. Morris, and G. Portelance. "Examining the Debt Implications of the Belt and Road Initiative from a Policy Perspective". CGD Policy Papers, no. 121, 2018.

Karlsrud, J. "From Liberal Peacebuilding to Stabilization and Counterterrorism". *International Peacekeeping*, vol. 26, no. 1, 2019, pp. 1–21, doi:10.1080/13533312.2018.1502040.

Legarda, H. (2018). "China as a Conflict Mediator: Maintaining Stability along the Belt and Road". MERICS China Mapping, 22 Aug. 2018.

Mansfield, E. D., and J. Snyder. "Democratization and the Danger of War". *International Security*, vol. 20, no. 1, 1995, pp. 5–38, doi:10.2307/2539213.

———. "Prone to Violence: The Paradox of the Democratic Peace". *The National Interest*, vol. 82, 2005, pp. 39–45.

Maoz, Z., and B. Russett. "Normative and Structural Causes of Democratic Peace, 1946–1986". *American Political Science Review*, vol. 87, no. 3, 1993, pp. 624–638, doi:10.2307/2938740.

Owen, J. M. "How Liberalism Produces Democratic Peace". *International Security*, vol. 19, no. 2, 1994, pp. 87–125, doi:10.2307/2539197.

Paris, R. "Saving Liberal Peacebuilding". *Review of International Studies*, vol. 36, no. 2, 2010, pp. 337–365, doi:10.1017/s0260210510000057.

Rachman, G. *Easternization: Asia's Rise and America's Decline from Obama to Trump and beyond*. Other Press, LLC, 2017.

Ray, D., and J. Esteban. "Conflict and Development". *Annual Review of Economics*, vol. 9, 2017, pp. 263–293.

Stahle, S. "China's Shifting Attitude towards United Nations Peacekeeping Operations". *China Quarterly*, vol. 195, 2008, pp. 631–655, doi:10.1017/s0305741008000805.

United Nations. *The Challenge of Sustaining Peace. Report of the Advisory Group of Experts for the 2015 Review of the United Nations Peacebuilding Architecture*. New York, United Nations, 2015.

———. *Peacebuilding and Sustaining Peace: Report of the Secretary-General*. New York, United Nations General Assembly, 2018.

———. *Uniting our Strengths for Peace: Politics, Partnerships and People. Report of the High-Level Independent Panel on United Nations Peace Operations*. New York, United Nations, 2015.

Vines, David, and Samuel Wills. "The Rebuilding Macroeconomic Theory Project: An Analytical Assessment". *Oxford Review of Economic Policy*, vol. 34, nos. 1–2, 2018, pp. 1–42.

Wang, X. "Developmental Peace: Understanding China's Africa Policy in Peace and Security". *China and Africa*, edited by Chris Alden et al., Springer, 2018, pp. 67–82.

World Bank and United Nations. *Pathways for Peace: Inclusive Approaches to Preventing Violent Conflict*. Washington, DC, World Bank, 2018.

Zhao, L. "Two Pillars of China's Global Peace Engagement Strategy: UN Peacekeeping and International Peacebuilding". *International Peacekeeping*, vol. 18, no. 3, 2011, pp. 344–362, doi:10.1080/13533312.2011.563107.

Zhao, M. "The BRI Is not a Debt Trap!". *CHINA-US Focus*, 16 Oct. 2018.

2 Political violence prevention
Definitions and implications

Stephanie C. Hofmann

Introduction

Not all conflict is bad. As others have pointed out,

> Conflict is the pursuit of contrary or seemingly incompatible
> interests – whether between individuals, groups or countries. It can
> be a major force for positive social change. In states with good gov-
> ernance, strong civil society and robust political and social systems
> where human rights are protected, conflicting interests are managed
> and ways found for groups to pursue their goals peacefully.
>
> (Department for International Development 6)

However, conflict can also turn violent. And violence rarely if ever
brings positive social change. In the last years, the number of violent
conflicts has risen again, as has the death toll (Uppsala Conflict Data
Program and International Peace Research Institute). People fear for
the violation of their human rights and their peaceful everyday exist-
ence as violent conflict destroys social and political relationships that
attempt to regulate "contrary or seemingly incompatible interests".

When intervening in (post-)conflicts – either in the form of military
or civilian peace operations or as humanitarian action – national, international, regional, transnational, or nongovernmental actors face many
constraints. First, actors' military or civilian resources are often costly
and/or scarce. Second, humanitarian, development, and security actors
often are required to commit for much longer than anticipated. A look
at the International Committee of the Red Cross (ICRC), for example,
reveals that the

> average length of time the ICRC has been present in the countries
> hosting its ten largest operations is more than 36 years. Protracted

conflicts are a major source of human suffering and a cause of protracted displacement, migration and development reversals.

(International Committee of the Red Cross 5)

Third, some actors more than others are selective as to where and how to intervene in violent conflict situations and follow political agendas not necessarily related to the conflict. This potentially jeopardizes other actors on the ground. Fourth, some actors and scholars have criticized foreign interventions as inappropriate measures to take – often lacking enough knowledge about the conflict in question (Englebert and Tull).

For all of these reasons and more, some (inter)national and transnational actors have introduced ideas and norms related to preventing violent conflict and sustaining peace to the agenda. Some have done so in more declaratory fashion, while others have established institutional capacities and devoted resources to the said goal. But what exactly do we mean by preventing conflict? And how can such ideas be operationalized and implemented? First, this brief discussion presents a few impressions that demonstrate that we are misnaming the phenomenon that should more accurately be called *prevention of violent conflict* or *political violence prevention*, not conflict prevention.[1] Second, while it feels intuitively right for many actors to want sustainable peace and to prevent violent conflict from happening (though we should not forget that some actors benefit from violence), prevention can be understood in different ways. And actors can be committed to prevention while pursuing different approaches. By broadening the concept to many different activities, any social interaction that tries to sustain or recreate peaceful relations can therefore be called an effort in preventing violent conflict from (re)emerging. This can overburden any actor. Given the different ideas that surround preventing violent conflict, it is important for actors to clearly define what they understand their primary purpose to be.[2] At the end of the day, we might need not a new concept to break out of organizational silos, but efficient on-the-ground coordination mechanisms to create more long-lasting stability and possibly peace.

Different ideas on how to prevent violent conflict

Ideas of how to prevent violent conflict – and maintain some sort of peace, though what kind of peace is not always spelled out – from happening, have existed for centuries. We can go back to Charles-Irénée Castel de Saint Pierre who in 1713 argued for the creation of an international organization to maintain peace. Saint Pierre influenced Kant who in 1795 argued that to establish perpetual peace, we need to focus on the republican constitution of states, their economic interdependence, and a cosmopolitan minded population (Doyle). For both of these scholars, the structural conditions between actors have to change before establishing and maintaining peaceful relations. Today, we often refer to this as *structural prevention* with an emphasis on legal arrangements and institutions.

More recent scholarship has looked into the different qualities of peace arrangements and has linked those to the potential of preventing violent conflict in the future. The eminent peace scholar Johan Galtung focuses on negative (absence of war) and positive (absence of war + elimination of structural inequalities) peace. Benjamin Miller emphasizes cold, normal, and warm peace (Miller). Either way, these scholars point out that if we think of different peace arrangements, then some (e.g. warm or positive peace) are most conducive to sustainable peace while others (e.g. cold or negative peace) are rather shallow and can lead to the resumption of violence (Mac Ginty). From this, it is only a small jump to argue that preventive diplomacy[3] is a necessary tool to address political tensions but that to establish warm or positive peace, it is insufficient without structural changes that address the conflict's root causes. In other words, preventing violent conflict can either be an end to halt political violence or to create conditions for lasting peace.

When the Carnegie Commission issued their report on *Preventing Deadly Conflict*, they reminded the international community that we should distinguish between operational and structural prevention. In the context of the report, operational prevention is not understood in terms of preventive diplomacy but defines operational approaches to violent conflict prevention such as addressing an ongoing or imminent escalation of violence (e.g. tools that can help identify at-risk demographics and develop targeted programs); structural approaches, on the other hand, take a longer-term view looking at the impact on broader societal structures.

There exist, of course, many more definitions that fit under "preventing violent conflict" but as this short discussion has shown, how peace is defined can impact both the definition and the operationalization (i.e. what kind of resources are made available) of preventing violent conflict. Not only this, but we should also wonder whether *preventing conflict* or *conflict prevention* are not misnomers. *Prevention of violent conflict* or *political violence prevention* might much better describe what UN Secretary-General António Guterres set out to do when he said in his remarks at a UN Security Council open debate on maintaining international peace and security on January 10, 2017: "Prevention is not merely a priority, but the priority". To address his agenda, he asked for a "whole new approach" which would at the same time connect existing efforts and break free of existing silos.

Normative developments and prevention

Ideas about how to prevent violent conflict from happening have existed for centuries, but, normatively speaking, many powerful actors were preoccupied with defending their territories or aggrandizing them, and therefore did not pick up on preventive diplomacy or violent conflict prevention. Only with international normative changes that started at the latest after World War II, with the development of more robust international treaties (e.g. defining international crimes or arguing when the use of force is appropriate), have national and international actors included aspects of violent conflict prevention in their resolutions and charters.

Normatively speaking, the emphasis still is primarily on interstate relations and the management of political violence rather than the prevention of it. Conflict prevention is often an afterthought in legal texts. The UN sees the use of force as only permissible in rare circumstances of self-defense (Art. 51 UN Charter). Otherwise, "all members shall refrain in their international relations from the threat or use of force against the territorial integrity or political independence of any state, or in any other manner inconsistent with the purposes of the United Nations" (Article 2 of the UN Charter). Instead, "all members shall settle their international disputes by peaceful means in such a manner that international peace and security, and justice, are not endangered" (Art. 2, UN Charter). Chapter VI of the UN Charter thereby outlines what measures member states can take to settle their conflicts peacefully: negotiation, inquiry, mediation, conciliation, arbitration, judicial settlement, or other peaceful means. If these measures are not successful and the United Nations Security Council (UNSC) determines that a threat to peace exists, it can order the use of force against a member state's will (Chapter VII UN Charter), including measures such as sanctions, embargoes, and the severance of diplomatic relations (Art. 41 and Art. 42 UN Charter) and military intervention (Art. 43–48 UN Charter).

Intrastate configurations and the protecting of individuals/ civilians have become more prominent in international and transnational debates after many violent intrastate conflicts and political disintegrations in the 1990s. Many states have reacted to these conflicts by calling for more guidance as to how to intervene in intrastate affairs. One such process has resulted in the formulation and grouping of a body of existing norms to form the "responsibility to protect". This norm complex reconfirms the states' and state-led organizations' role in preventing political violence, by protecting citizens and rebuilding social institutions in the interest of peaceful relations. The protection of civilians has become an important normative pillar as well. However, these normative developments do not emphasize prevention as much as the reduction of political violence and the establishing of stability after conflict has happened.

Raising questions about political violence prevention

The ideas and normative developments are closely linked to the questions of what exactly should be prevented and how actors want to prevent it from happening. Decisions have to be made as to when and how long to engage. One set of questions relates to decisions about prioritization of certain factors: How much consideration should be given to systemic factors that can contribute to violent conflict? Does one want to prevent the immediate threat of physical violence and is there a threshold that would trigger such action? Do intervening actors see monitoring the situation (either from afar or up close, i.e. first, second, or third generation early warning systems) as the main task? Should the intervention have as a goal to stabilize the (poten-tial) conflict situation (e.g. through the establishment of dispute reso-lution mechanisms of mediation efforts) or are other political goals such as democratization also envisaged (e.g. by strengthening a par-ticular interpretation of the rule of law)? Is it "enough" to address triggers or should so-called root causes also be included in a pre-vention policy? How do we know whether the root causes are really the root?

Another set of questions that should be taken into consideration is the potential unintended consequences of intervening activities: Under what conditions do international interventions prolong pol-itical violence? By calling activities "preventing conflict" are we not already reconfirming conflicting lines instead of overcoming them? And how can we make sure that prevention is not being used to justify preventive war?

And a third set of questions is about feasibility: What kind of activ-ities are actors willing to commit to, or capable of committing to? Is early warning what we need in situations where reporting is going on all over the world, i.e. we know of tensions but sometimes do not know how to interpret them sufficiently? Aggravating the issue of focusing on potential root causes is that conflict dynamics could have changed cleavage patterns to such a degree that root causes are hard to identify.

Implementing political violence prevention: conceptual ambiguities and organizational turfs

As the last sections have shown, in conceiving a policy to prevent political violence from happening, many conceptual, normative, and operational choices have to be made. When we look at international organizations as well as their mandates and activities, we see that "conflict prevention" or "preventive diplomacy" are not simply ideas but comprehensive concepts that contain, generate, and sustain many processes, approaches, and stages needed to prevent political violence from (re) emerging. While many international organizations have been created to prevent the recurrence of violence (Haftel and Hofmann) among and/or outside their membership, concrete policies have often been formulated later (Ackermann). Today, most international organizations with trade, development, and security mandates not only have included the goal of sustaining peace among their membership in their treaties and declarations but also have developed institutional structures and capabilities to do so. In the UN family alone, various agencies see themselves active in this domain. Next to them, regional organizations have also set out to take issues related to political violence prevention on board.

These organizations often understand the prevention of political violence from their bureaucratic and political silos (Hofmann). Organizational actors who have been working on issues that can be framed as "political violence prevention" but might organizationally be called peacebuilding, conflict management, or sustainable peace, do not necessarily want to give up responsibilities when a "new" concept needs to be operationalized and implemented. I will briefly mention a few organizational conceptualizations and activities that fall under political violence prevention to demonstrate operational overlap and ambiguities. The outline below should be understood schematically as it does not give enough credit to organizational activities and changes over time.

The United Nations

UN language oscillates between preventive diplomacy, conflict prevention, and an agenda for sustaining peace – closely interrelated concepts that nonetheless bear different politics. These different concepts have different constituencies within the UN system, which creates conceptual boundary issues and implementation responsibilities. The *Agenda for Peace* called for fact-finding and analysis-to identify at the earliest possible stage the circumstances that could produce serious conflict – and the need for Preventive Diplomacy to resolve the most immediate problems with attention to underlying causes of conflict. The 2001 *Report of the Secretary-General on Prevention of Armed Conflict* (United Nations General Assembly) called for "an effective preventive strategy" which requires "a comprehensive approach that encompasses both short-term and long-term political, diplomatic, humanitarian, human rights, developmental, institutional, and other measures taken by the international community, in cooperation with national and regional actors". And a Statement by the President of the Security Council in January 2018 reads "The Security Council further recalls that a comprehensive conflict prevention strategy should include, inter alia, early warning, preventive deployment, mediation, peacekeeping, non-proliferation, accountability measures as well as post-conflict peacebuilding, and recognizes that these components are interdependent, complementary, and non-sequential."

The United Nations Development Programme, for example, engages less with conceptual innovations than with adapting new concepts to their already ongoing activities. Its understanding of preventing conflict is end-driven. "UNDP's work on conflict prevention promotes social cohesion by empowering nations and communities to become inclusive and resilient to external and internal shocks. This is done by supporting and strengthening key relevant governance institutions" (United Nations Development Programme).

The United Nations and the World Bank

An inter-organizational report between the World Bank and the UN, *Pathways for Peace – Inclusive Approaches to Preventing Violent Conflict*, includes many different activities and actors when considering conflict prevention. It is one of the first texts published by international organizations that emphasized that not only states are responsible in preventing violent conflict. The report stresses "activities aimed at preventing the outbreak, escalation, continuation and recurrence of conflict, addressing root causes, assisting parties to conflict to end hostilities, ensuring national reconciliation and moving towards recovery, reconstruction, and development" (World Bank and United Nations 77). It is, as such, more people-oriented and advocates an integrated and proactive approach. It furthermore adds a further dimension to violent conflict prevention (next to structural and operational): systemic prevention.

The African Union

After its inception in 2002, the African Union established a Conflict Prevention and Early Warning Division whose mandate is

> to provide timely advice on potential conflicts and threats to peace and security in Africa to the AU decision-makers. The Division focuses on the operationalization of some aspects of the African Peace and Security Architecture (APSA) including the Continental Early Warning System (CEWS), the Panel of the Wise (PoW) and the AU Border Programme (AUBP).

The AU thereby tries to include the Early Warning Systems of African subregional organizations (based on a Memorandum of Understanding in 2008). While it is still in the process of building structures that could be used for both preventive diplomacy and more comprehensive violent conflict prevention, pundits observe that "Currently, the AU's focus is on conflict prevention through initiatives such as diplomacy efforts and mediation" (de Carvalho 3).

The Association of Southeast Asian Nations and ASEAN Regional Forum

The Southeast and East Asian UN member states are inclined to refrain from the concept of conflict prevention and rather stress confidence-building and consensual and noncoercive preventive diplomacy.[4] ASEAN, the ASEAN Regional Forum (ARF), and various ASEAN-Plus arrangements (such as ASEAN + 8) are institutional structures to be used for these ends. Under Article 32 (c) of the ASEAN Charter, the chairman shall "ensure an effective and timely response to urgent issues or crisis situations affecting ASEAN, including providing its good offices and such other arrangements to immediately address these concerns". In other words,

> Preventive diplomacy in Southeast Asia has been defined narrowly to minimize the role for those outside the region and to reinforce ASEAN's strong doctrine of non-interference in the internal affairs of member countries. It marginalizes other multilateral institutions and excludes nongovernmental organizations. ARF defines preventive diplomacy as any diplomatic or political action taken by

states to prevent disputes or conflicts that could threaten regional peace and stability, to prevent such disputes from escalating into armed confrontation, or to minimize the impact of such conflicts on the region.

(Della-Giacoma)

Della-Giacoma continues by outlining the eight key principles of preventive diplomacy, which are that it

(i) uses peaceful methods such as negotiation, enquiry, mediation, and conciliation; (ii) is noncoercive; (iii) is timely; (iv) requires trust and confidence; (v) involves consultation and consensus; (vi) is voluntary; (vii) applies to direct conflict between states; and (viii) is conducted in accordance with international law.

(Della-Giacoma)

An ARF document entitled *Concept and Principles of Preventive Diplomacy* (PD) even points out that

agreement on the definition and, more importantly, a common understanding of the concept of PD and the principles governing the practice of PD, would be useful for further progress on the development of PD within the ARF ... the definition has proven to be controversial.

No full and concrete mechanism for fostering preventive diplomacy has been institutionalized yet.

The European Union

The EU can be considered a political violence prevention initiative itself. After World War II, it was created to avoid conflict in the future. Next to this, it has many institutional frameworks and tools at hand to engage in political violence prevention.

The EU external action for the prevention of conflicts is based on: Early identification of risk of violent conflict, and closing the gap to early action; Improved understanding of conflict situations (root causes, actors and dynamics); Enhanced identification of the range of options for EU action; Conflict-sensitive programming of external assistance ... Mediation is part of the EU's on-the-ground preventive diplomacy and is a component of the EU's conflict prevention and peace-building toolbox for conflict countries.

(European External Action Service)

Member states, and in particular those who operate in Sub-Saharan Africa under the EU umbrella, push the EU to provide military assistance as part of its violence prevention policies. In other words, the EU understands and enacts political violence prevention through the diplomatic, development, and security lenses. These different approaches are not coordinated under a single institutional umbrella, however.

Political violence prevention involves many actors and coordination is hard to come by, even if these actors are all located in one and the same international organization. Within the EU, prevention is the responsibility of different actors and instruments across the EU's external action remits. Security, development, and human rights might be conceptually interlinked but this does not make them automatically mutually reinforcing. For the EU, what this means in practice is that political violence prevention is situated in the Commission, the European External Action Service and the Council as well as member states, while foreign policy, security, development, and humanitarian agendas are kept apart. In addition, within the organization, these institutional set ups have often not only responded to "needs" but also been based on institutional logics and turf wars. Talk today about fragility and resilience, for example, is also a way to give the European Commission some operational turf back.[5]

The Organization for Security and Cooperation in Europe

The OSCE sees itself as a "key instrument for early warning, conflict prevention and resolution, crisis management and post-conflict rehabilitation" (Organization for Security and Cooperation in Europe). One of its main tools to achieve conflict prevention is its Conflict Prevention Centre which serves as "an OSCE-wide early warning focal point, facilitates dialogue, supports mediation and other conflict preventions and resolution efforts". In addition, it supports field missions. As with some other organizations, early warning is a cornerstone of preventing violent conflict and the organization is more process- than end-oriented.

As this brief eclectic selection of international organizations illustrates, not all international organizations understand and act upon the prevention of political violence in the same way. They furthermore do not always sit easily with the UN or other regional frameworks that also want to intervene in the same geographical space. Last but not least, they vary significantly in their institutional capacity in terms of tools and resources. In short, political violence prevention is operationalized differently in different international organizations depending on their organizational structures and normative priorities (e.g. noninterference, human rights, development, stability); this makes an assessment of success – which is hard in any case – even harder.

Conclusion

Policies that could be framed as political violence prevention have already existed in different cloths such as peacebuilding or development. Consequently, the resurgent interest in preventing political violence encroaches on policy and operational turfs that are arguably already institutionalized. Hence, actors who subscribe to the prevention of political violence should first take stock of current institutional infrastructures and assess whether new resources and capacities are needed to tackle the challenge. Actors should ask themselves what needs to happen for these existing mechanisms so that they become "preventive". Before coming up with new tools and more sophisticated early warning systems (some of which have already been developed and used before the conflict prevention discourse became *en vogue*), it would be good to evaluate what has worked and what has not worked and why. In any case, the reinvigoration of concepts alone is not enough to create a policy. Normative concepts, mechanisms, resources, and capacities need to be attached to such concepts.

Next to monitoring and evaluating existing programs, it might be good to consider establishing and reinforcing existing coordination and evaluation mechanisms for international organizations active in the same geographical space – if possible, for example, as a joint or coordinated strategic review process. These review processes should encourage inclusive narratives of institutional failures so that lessons can be learned. As it stands, the many actors can challenge coordination and quality control, duplicate each other's efforts, and even unintentionally undermine each other's violence reduction attempts. For example, one danger on the ground is that of creating violent conflict prevention fatigue among local actors. International stakeholders constantly invite local officials, civil society representatives, etc. to workshops, trainings, and forums without necessarily assessing local needs or considering local priorities.

This is not to say that actors should automatically link up to more integrated, comprehensive, or holistic approaches (e.g. the development–security nexus). Looking for comparative advantages and establishing partnerships that clearly define these comparative advantages helps create buy-in. It is also important to share, but to not align conflict analysis tools as well as with local stakeholders, and to encourage local narratives. This way, we do not assess violence potentials according to templates but open a space for discussion that helps assess political situations. Conflict analysis is a necessary but highly insufficient condition for conflict sensitivity in any case. Regular monitoring of international actors' activities, regular consultation with a broad group of stakeholders, as well as ongoing adjustment of the activities and, possibly, their aims are also necessary. This way, actors invite in more narratives of what could constitute success, impact, and performance.

Notes

1 Let alone its conceptual boundary issues with other terms such as conflict transformation or peacebuilding.
2 The same applies to conflict. For example, several datasets that all claim to measure conflict use different indicators to empirically determine when they see conflict.
3 Of this term, the UN has said,

> Since Dag Hammarskjöld first articulated the concept over half a century ago, it has continued to evolve in response to new challenges. An integral part of broader conflict prevention efforts, preventive diplomacy refers specially to diplomatic action taken, at the earliest possible stage, "to prevent disputes from arising between parties, to prevent existing disputes from escalating into conflicts and to limit the spread of the latter when they occur".
>
> (United Nations)

4 It is interesting to note that when the UN and ASEAN meet to discuss the issue of preventing conflict, the meeting takes place under both conflict prevention and preventive diplomacy headings; see for example "ASEAN-UN talks" (Ng).
5 Similar dynamics can be observed if we look at peacebuilding activities within the UN system. One can just hope that competition in the short term can be good as this might increase organizations' turf and innovation capacity as they have to argue for their *raison d'être*.

Bibliography

Ackermann, Alice. "The Idea and Practice of Conflict Prevention". *Journal of Peace Research*, vol. 40, no. 3, 2003, pp. 339–347.

African Union. *Conflict Prevention and Early Warning Division of the AU Peace and Security Department*. 2018, www.peaceau.org/uploads/conflict-prevention-and-early-warning-booklet-13feb18-approved.pdf.

ASEAN Regional Forum (ARF). "Concept and Principles of Preventive Diplomacy". ARF, http://aseanregionalforum.asean.org/wp-content/uploads/2019/01/ARF-Concept-Paper-of-Preventive-Diplomacy.pdf, no date.

Carnegie Commission. *Preventing Deadly Conflict*. 1997, www.carnegie.org/publications/preventing-deadly-conflict-final-report/.

de Carvalho, Gustavo. "Conflict Prevention. What's In It for the AU?" ISS Policy Briefs, Institute for Security Studies and Training for Peace, 2017, https://issafrica.s3.amazonaws.com/site/uploads/policybrief103-2.pdf.

Della-Giacoma, Jim. "Preventive Diplomacy in Southeast Asia: Redefining the ASEAN Way". International Peace Institute, 2011, www.crisisgroup.org/asia/south-east-asia/preventive-diplomacy-southeast-asia-redefining-asean-way.

Department for International Development. "Preventing Violent Conflict". DFID Policy Papers, 2007, https://reliefweb.int/report/world/dfid-policy-paper-preventing-violent-conflict.

Doyle, Michael W. "Liberalism and World Politics". *American Political Science Review*, vol. 80, no. 4, 1986, pp. 1151–1170.

Englebert, Pierre, and Denis M. Tull. "Postconflict Reconstruction in Africa: Flawed Ideas about Failed States". *International Security*, vol. 32, no. 4, 2008, pp. 106–139.

European External Action Service. "Conflict Prevention, Peace building and Mediation". 2017, https://eeas.europa.eu/headquarters/headquarters-homepage/426/conflict-prevention-peace-building-and-mediation_en.

Galtung, Johan. "Violence, Peace and Peace Research". *Journal of Peace Research*, vol. 6, no. 3, 1969, pp. 167–191.

Haftel, Yoram, and Stephanie C. Hofmann. "Institutional Authority and Security Cooperation within Regional Economic Organizations". *Journal of Peace Research*, vol. 54, no. 4, 2017, pp. 484–498.

Hofmann, Stephanie C. "The Politics of Overlapping Organizations: Hostage-Taking, Forum Shopping, and Brokering". *Journal of European Public Policy*, vol. 26, no. 6, 2019, pp. 803–905, www.tandfonline.com/doi/full/10.1080/13501763.2018.1512644.

International Committee of the Red Cross. *Protracted Conflict and Humanitarian Action: Some Recent ICRC Experiences*. Geneva, International Committee of the Red Cross, 2016, www.icrc.org/sites/default/files/document/file_list/protracted_conflict_and_humanitarian_action_icrc_report_lr_29.08.16.pdf.

Mac Ginty, Roger. "Hybrid Peace: The Interaction between Top-Down and Bottom-Up Peace". *Security Dialogue*, vol. 41, no. 4, 2010, pp. 391–412.

Miller, Benjamin. "Explaining Variations in Regional Peace: Three Strategies for Peace-Making". *Cooperation and Conflict*, vol. 35, no. 2, 2000, pp. 155–192.

Ng, Swan Ti. "ASEAN-UN Talks Focus on Conflict Prevention and Preventive Diplomacy". Association of Southeast Asian Nations, 5 Apr. 2013, http://asean.org/asean-un-talks-focus-on-conflict-prevention-and-preventive-diplomacy/.

Organization for Security and Cooperation in Europe. "Conflict prevention and resolution". www.osce.org/conflict-prevention-and-resolution.

United Nations. *Charter of the United Nations, and Statute of the International Court of Justice*. https://www.un.org/en/charter-united-nations/.

———. "Preventive Diplomacy: Delivering Results". *Report of the Secretary-General*, UN Doc. S/2011/552, 2011, www.un.org/undpa/sites/www.un.org.undpa/files/SG%20Report%20on%20Preventive%20Diplomacy.pdf.

———. "Statement by the President of the Security Council". S/PRST/2018/1, 2018.

United Nations Development Programme. "Democratic Governance and Peacebuilding". 2018, www.undp.org/content/undp/en/home/democratic-governance-and-peacebuilding/conflict-prevention.html.

United Nations General Assembly. "Prevention of Armed Conflict". *Report of the Secretary-General*, UN Doc. A/55/985-S/2001/574, 2001, http://unpan1.un.org/intradoc/groups/public/documents/un/unpan005902.pdf.

United Nations Secretary-General. "An Agenda for Peace". *Report of the Secretary-General*, UN Doc. A/42/277, 1992, www.un-documents.net/a47-277.htm.

Uppsala Conflict Data Program and International Peace Research Institute. *UCDP/PRIO Armed Conflict Dataset Codebook*. PRIO, 2013.

World Bank and United Nations. *Pathways for Peace: Inclusive Approaches to Preventing Violence Conflict*. World Bank, 2018.

3 A tale of two "peaces"

Liberal peace, developmental peace, and peacebuilding

*Yin He**

Introduction

As China's overall national strength keeps increasing apace, its role in global governance is now a heated topic. At the same time, President Xi Jinping has expressed strong willingness to actively participate in reform of the global governance system. In the light of such a background, China is no longer merely an ordinary participant in many important global affairs, but also a core actor, as China's international identity has expanded from a norm taker to a norm contributor. As the largest inter-governmental organization, the United Nations (UN) is one of the key actors in global governance as well as the most important platform for international politics. For the past four decades, China's increasingly active participation in global affairs and integration into the international community has to a large extent been reflected in its participation in UN affairs, most notably peacekeeping (He "China's Doctrine" 110). Therefore, research into China's normative contribution to the UN peacekeeping regime can aid understanding of China's changing role in global governance.

As many UN peacekeeping operations established in the post-Cold War era now emphasize peacebuilding, this chapter will discuss China's normative contributions in that area. The major questions to be answered include: What is the Chinese norm of peacebuilding? And what will happen when the Chinese norm encounters the existing dominant peacebuilding norm?

Peacebuilding

In multi-dimensional peacekeeping operations, while working hard to secure a peaceful operational environment, peacekeepers and their civilian colleagues are authorized to conduct various peacebuilding activities, such as helping host states establish or reform political, economic, and social institutions, and building infrastructure. With such a background, the term "peacekeeping operation" is redefined, with these operations focusing on peacebuilding, which has become an important part of the efforts by the international community to maintain peace and security since the end of the Cold War.

The term "peacebuilding" was first proposed by Galtung in 1970, and by it he meant addressing the root causes of conflict and supporting local capacity for peace management and conflict resolution (Galtung "Three Approaches to Peace" 282–304). Peacebuilding became a familiar concept within the UN following Secretary-General Boutros Boutros-Ghali's 1992 report, *An Agenda for Peace*, which defined peacebuilding as actions to solidify peace and avoid relapsing into conflict (55–59). The *Supplement to an Agenda for Peace* published in 1995 by the UN Secretariat stressed the importance of building state institutions (Boutros-Ghali 47–56). Another milestone document for peacebuilding is the *Report of the Panel on United Nations Peace Operations* (also known as the "Brahimi Report") put forward by the UN Secretariat, which redefines peacebuilding as activities undertaken in post-conflict settings to reassemble the foundations of peace and to provide the tools for building something that is more than just the absence of the war (*Report of the Panel* 5). In 2005, the UN began to establish a peacebuilding architecture which has three institutional components: the United Nations Peacebuilding Commission, the Peacebuilding Fund, and the Peacebuilding Support Office (Jenkins 44–73). The institutional complex serves as an important platform for the UN and international community to help build sustainable peace in post-conflict societies. In 2015, the Secretary-General's Advisory Group of Experts submitted *The Challenges of Sustaining Peace: Report of the Advisory Group of Experts for the 2015 Review of the United Nations Peacebuilding Architecture*, which redefines "peacebuilding" and introduces a broader approach, "sustaining peace". According to the review, the concept of sustaining peace is supposed to liberate peacebuilding from the strict limitation to post-conflict contexts (17).

Besides this conceptual evolution and institutional development, another important part of peacebuilding is its activities and guiding norms. Since the early 1990s, UN peacebuilding has had an institutional focus. Prolonged violent conflicts usually gravely damage institutions. It is widely believed within the international peacebuilding community that strong institutions are the pre-requisite for efforts to build lasting peace. Therefore, there has been a focus on rebuilding and reinforcing the resilience of key institutions (*Challenges of Sustaining Peace* 17). More importantly, all peacebuilding activities are required to be done according to democratic rules and principles. In other words, a peace norm called "liberal peace" has prevailed in peacebuilding discourse and practice (Paris *At War's End*; Mac Ginty and Richmond).

Liberal peace and its limitations

Liberal peace derives from the practices of Western Civilization, with Western Europe and North America as its center. The liberal peace norm has two fundamental elements: liberalization and democratization, from which Western states have benefited greatly. For centuries past, due to its economic and military strength, the West has enjoyed an advantageous position on the international stage and has been able to export its values and political ideology to other parts of the world, playing a dominant role in shaping the international system. Under such conditions, the liberal peace is promoted as a universal peace norm and has influenced peacebuilding within the UN peace and security architecture and beyond.

Advocates of liberal peace believe that the most important task of peacebuilding in a post-conflict state is to establish democratic political institutions as well as neoliberal economic institutions. As a result, over the last three decades, a rough template seems to have emerged for international responses to post-conflict challenges (*Challenges of Sustaining Peace* 18): usually within a year or so after international intervention is initiated, a popular election is held, followed by various capacity-building and security sector reform efforts according to liberal democratic standards. At the same time, neoliberal economic institutions are set up with help – and pressure – from the international financial organizations such as the World Bank and the International Monetary Fund. Roland Paris's study shows that although the 14 peacebuilding operations established from 1989 to 1999 vary in many respects, they have some similarity: all of them had sought to transform war-torn states into liberal democracies. Paris asserts that liberal peace embodies a hypothesis: liberalization of political and economic institutions can lead to self-sustaining peace (*At War's End* 5).

However, liberal peacebuilding has two major limitations. One is that peacebuilding is dominated by a narrow statebuilding agenda. According to Oliver P. Richmond and Jason Franks, statebuilding aims at building a neoliberal, Weberian state with a clearly defined sovereign territory, and with a focus on political, economic, and security structure; peacebuilding, on the other hand, has a broader set of tasks ranging from individual needs and rights to community and governance structures (182). With statebuilding in the name of peacebuilding becoming the core task of multi-dimensional peacekeeping operations in the post–Cold War era, the result has been that these operations focus attention on addressing a small part of the long list of challenges of post-conflict states.

Another limitation of liberal peacebuilding is that it lacks inclusiveness. Any institutions or activities which are regarded as non-liberal or non-democratic will be rejected or excluded in order to transform the post-conflict state into a Western-style liberal democracy. Western donors play an important role in promoting liberal peace. They often attach political conditions to their aid in order to force the peacebuilding host states to reform their political and economic institutions according to liberal democratic standards. More, liberal peace promotes building a strong civil society and plays down the role of state government in economic and social affairs.

However, the "one size fits all" peace approach has a mixed record. After 9/11, US efforts to rebuild Iraq and Afghanistan descended into chaos, provoking debates over the liberal peace model of peacebuilding. Some believe that democratic political institutions and neoliberal economic institutions combined may cause political disorder, social tension, and even inter-ethnic violence (Chua). The peace built by liberal peace is a "virtual peace" (Newman et al.; Campbell et al.). These debates about the benefits of the liberal peace fall into two camps: "critical voices" and "problem solvers".

"Critical voices" range from challenges to the ideological core of liberal peace to doubts about its functions. Advocates of liberal peace promote the "democratic peace thesis", which argues that states with free markets and democratic politics do not go to war. This belief or assumption sets a good excuse for liberal international intervention including peacebuilding because liberal peace benefits not only the domestic affairs of post-conflict states, but also international peace and security in a broad sense. However, some are not so optimistic. For example, Roger MacGinty sharply points out that the "democratic peace thesis" is "complete rubbish", for "liberal states are regularly involved in confrontations with states they deem non-liberal, often under label of 'rogue', 'failed', or 'evil'" (40). Other critical voices against liberal peace focus on the effectiveness and result of peacebuilding. Some believe that peacebuilding has been reduced to a narrow statebuilding agenda (Reilly 113; Richmond and Franks 182). The result is that although many people in the UN system and international community have an original good intention to help post-conflict states build self-sustaining peace, in reality their comprehensive peacebuilding programs focus on building liberal democratic Weberian states. In other words, institution building has become the narrower, core task of peacebuilding. As Roland Paris notes, frustration at America's "regime change" invasion of Iraq contributed to a mounting backlash against all forms of liberal interventionism including UN-sponsored peacebuilding. Some discuss liberal interventionism as "hubristic and delusional" (Paris "Critiques of Liberal Peace" 38).

Although the critical voices can be helpful for one to understand the flaws of liberal peace, they have failed to propose useful alternatives and help solve the problems in peacebuilding. Some commentators have made efforts to provide concrete suggestions to improve liberal peace-oriented peacebuilding. They are called "problem solvers" here. Like critical voices, problem solvers too recognize many of the pitfalls of liberal peace. However, unlike most critical voices, who usually have very pessimistic views about liberal peace, problem solvers are more or less optimistic that the existing liberal peace–oriented peacebuilding can be improved. Some problem-solving approaches seek to revise the shortcomings of liberal peace intervention by redistributing power, including enhancing local responsibility and encouraging local ownership. Paris proposes changing the sequence of tasks. He suggests an approach of "institutionalization before liberalization" ("Alternatives to Liberal Peace" 163–164). Paris thinks that elections should be postponed until there has been a deeper instauration of associated institutions which will stabilize the environment for elections and render them more than symbolic exercises with only limited meaning and impact (Mac Ginty 26). In all, however, problem solvers tend to limit themselves to technical improvements without doubting the foundation of liberal peace. According to Paris, there is no realistic alternative to some form of liberal peacebuilding strategy at all ("Alternatives to Liberal Peace" 159).

As mentioned above, liberal peace derives from Western civilization. It is by nature a norm with regional characteristics. Due to the West's dominance and hegemony in the international power configuration and institutional regime, liberal peace has been promoted to become an international norm. The rise of China will undoubtedly lead to opportunities for China to influence the norms of global governance, including peacebuilding (Li and Peng; Ikenberry).

The rise of China and developmental peace

China's rise tells a peace story different from that of the West. To understand this, one should first understand the myth of China's rise: Why has China succeeded? Some try to answer this question from a political perspective, attributing China's success to "authoritarian government" and a "whole nation system" (*juguo tizhi*). Some try to answer this question from an economic perspective, arguing that the most important reason is that China is a Keynesian state. The government plays a leading role in economic affairs through investing in infrastructure and keeps the economic system under firm control by strengthening state-owned enterprises (SOEs). Some note that China's efforts to reform political institutions have also contributed to its success (Eric X. Li 56–57). Each of these views explains China's success from certain perspectives, and thus fails to present a full picture.

A rising power always promotes a zeitgeist: the United Kingdom promoted free trade and the United States promotes freedom and democracy (Zheng). The zeitgeist that the rising China promotes is peace and development, which was recognized and written into China's Constitution in 1992 as a guiding principle for its reform and opening up strategy. To China, peace, especially internal peace, is the most critical pre-requisite for development. The late architect of China's reform and opening up strategy, Premier Deng Xiaoping, insisted that internal stability should be secured at any cost. With a peaceful or stable political and social environment, China can make good use of its limited resources to implement the "economic development–oriented strategy". It believes in the Marxist philosophy of materialism that the economic foundation defines superstructure. To China, many social and political conflicts can find their root causes in underdevelopment. In other words, successful national development, with economic development as the foundation, is the solution to conflicts and key to the door of peace.

The experience of China's rise can be summarized as a norm called "developmental peace". Like liberal peace, developmental peace too embodies a hypothesis: with political and social stability as a pre-requisite, development can lead to sustainable peace. Even though China does not have any official agenda to promote developmental peace, the norm has begun to exert influence internationally through China's increasing international aid and economic activities, including in the field of peacebuilding (He "United Nations Peacebuilding" 91).

A comparison of the two "peaces"

Both liberal peace and developmental peace are peacebuilding norms. As is shown in Table 3.1, they differ greatly in many ways. In terms of origin, the two peace norms derive from two different civilizations and have different practice foundations. Difference in origin also means that the two peace norms are based on different value patterns and philosophic systems.

Besides normal economic activities, aid is an important way for external actors to assist in the peacebuilding process of post-conflict states. When Western countries give aid to peacebuilding host countries, they will usually attach a liberal peace package, setting strict political conditions. For example, they may require the aid recipient countries to reform their political and economic institutions according to liberal democratic standards. They may also want aid recipient countries to lower their tariffs and privatize SOEs. However, unlike the Western countries, China does not attach political conditions to its aid to other countries (Brautigam 76).

The two peace norms have different priorities: liberal peace attaches the greatest importance to institution building while developmental peace gives priority to economic development. This difference is very critical because to post-conflict states, resources for peacebuilding can be very limited, especially at the early stage of peacebuilding. Different top priorities may lead to different results from peacebuilding.

Liberal peace prefers a small government, insisting that strong civil society like non-governmental actors should be encouraged and empowered to participate in governance and provide public services. However, developmental peace prefers a big government and downplays the role of civil society, insisting that the government should play a leading role in a state's political, economic, and social affairs. Liberal peace advocates fundamentalist rules of market economy, opposing interference in market activities from the state government. Developmental peace recognizes the role of market, too; but it insists that the state government should keep its economic affairs under control through macro-control measures such as strengthening SOEs and guiding investment in public areas including infrastructure (Lin 5–10).

Table 3.1 Comparison of the two peace norms in peacebuilding

Comparison aspects	Liberal peace	Developmental peace
Origin	Western civilization	Chinese civilization
Political conditions for aid	Yes	No
Top priority	Institution building	Economic development
Role of government	Small	Big
Transformation approach	Radical	Gradual
Governance model	Good governance	Effective governance
Diffusion strategy	Teaching	Imitating and learning

When it comes to pace of transformation, liberal peace often advocates radical change. Many post-conflict states are required to abandon their non-liberal and non-democratic institutions and practices, and accept reform packages or "shock therapy". Developmental peace opposes radical change or a "one size fits all" approach. It believes that every state has its own conditions; therefore, reform should be done gradually through "wading across the stream by feeling the way" (*mozhe shitou guohe*). Liberal peace is a value-based norm. It promotes good governance, limiting governance rules and practices to a Western standard. Developmental peace is a non-value-based and inclusive norm. It promotes effective governance, welcoming any governance rules and practices that can contribute to peace and development.

Finally, the two peace norms are diffused in different ways. Liberal peace has many advocates, including the Western states and their international development institutions, the United Nations, international financial organizations, and international non-governmental organizations. These actors believe that if post-conflict states want to build lasting peace, they must accept liberal peace. Therefore, liberal peace is usually taught to host countries. Although the new Chinese leadership under President Xi Jinping has shown confidence in providing "Chinese approaches" to global governance, so far China has not promoted any Chinese normative package internationally. Some leading Chinese academics hold that China's rise has not generated any universal norms (Junru Li 14). In other words, although many elements of developmental peace have been demonstrated in China's international aid and economic activities including the Belt and Road Initiative, the peace norm has not been endorsed by the Chinese government or the Chinese aid community. Nevertheless, developing countries, including those post-conflict ones, cannot be prevented from imitating and learning China's experience as well as practice in economic, political, and social development.

A case study of when the two "peaces" meet: peacebuilding in East Timor

Although liberal peace and developmental peace differ greatly, what is happening in peacebuilding proves that many post-conflict states have enough room to accommodate both peace norms. An in-depth analysis of the two peacebuilding processes of Haiti and Liberia shows that the effect of the peacebuilding in Liberia, where the two peace norms coexist and compete with each other, is comparatively much better than that in Haiti, where "liberal peace" dominates the whole peacebuilding process while "developmental peace" cannot play a significant role (He "Norm Competition" 116–121).

An exploration of the process and result of the peacebuilding in East Timor can even better reflect the relationship between the two peace norms. From 1999 to 2012, the UN had established a series of peacekeeping operations in East Timor. Since the UN exited from East Timor in 2012, the country has appeared to be walking on a road of sustainable peace. The UN regards East Timor as one of few successful cases of peacebuilding (*Challenges of Sustaining Peace* 18). One of the main reasons for the success is that East Timor's peacebuilding has accommodated both liberal peace and developmental peace.

When building institutions, although East Timor has to a large extent embraced liberal peace, it has not adopted confrontational democracy. Instead, East Timor has turned to consensus democracy, which provides a platform to include a wide range of political forces and avoid unnecessary waste of limited resources. For example, consensus democracy has helped to unite the limited number of East Timorese elites, most of whom are veteran politicians grown up during the revolutionary struggle against the Indonesian occupation before independence. Although veteran politicians like Xanana Gusmao and José Ramos-Horta took power in turn, these "old men" of politics contributed significantly to unite the young state and maintain political and social stability (He "Developmental Peace" 29–30).

As there is a stable political and social environment, East Timor can allocate most of its limited resources to development. A strong central government makes it possible for the young state to effectively manage its economic affairs. Political stability also secures continuity of policy and allows East Timor to make a long-term economic development plan. With effective governance, East Timor has successfully avoided a "resource curse" that bothers many resource rich countries, setting up a sovereign wealth fund with the revenue generated from the oil and gas in the Timor Sea. The success of peacebuilding in East Timor also shows that liberal peace and developmental peace can coexist and forge complementary relations, making a joint contribution to peacebuilding (He "Developmental Peace" 29–30).

Conclusion

As there are many challenges in peacebuilding for post-conflict states, any one dominant peace paradigm alone cannot help to build lasting peace. Peacebuilding has two most critical tasks: institution building and economic development, both of which are indispensable for building sustainable peace. Therefore, in practice, there exists no logic that one is more urgent than another.

Liberal peace and developmental peace derive from different patterns of practice of two great civilizations, and they have different ideological concepts as well as normative contents. Nevertheless, both of them have advantages over each other in addressing certain challenges in peacebuilding in post-conflict states. Generally speaking, liberal peace is more concerned with institution building than development, while developmental peace more effectively helps with economic development than does liberal peace. Their coexistence can greatly benefit peacebuilding in post-conflict states. Peacebuilding in the twenty-first century will be a tale of two "peaces".

Note

* Yin He is Associate Professor at the China Peacekeeping Police Training Center (CPPTC). The views expressed in this chapter are those of the author and do not represent any stance of the CPPTC or the Chinese Ministry of Public Security.

Bibliography

Boutros-Ghali, Boutros. *An Agenda for Peace: Preventive Diplomacy, Peacemaking and Peacekeeping*. United Nations, 17 June 1992, www.un.org. Accessed 12 Dec. 2018.

———. *Supplement to an Agenda for Peace: Position Paper of Secretary-General on Occasion of the Fiftieth Anniversary of the United Nations: Report of the Secretary-General on the Work of the Organization*. United Nations, 15 Sept. 1997, www.un.org. Accessed 12 Dec. 2018.

Brautigam, Deborah. *The Dragon's Gift: The Real Story of China in Africa*. Oxford UP, 2009.

Campbell, Susana, et al., editors. *A Liberal Peace? The Problems and Practices of Peacebuilding*. Zed Books, 2011.

The Challenges of Sustaining Peace: Report of the Advisory Group of Experts for the 2015 Review of the United Nations Peacebuilding Architecture. United Nations, 17 June 2015, www.un.org/en/ga/search/view_doc.asp?symbol=S/2015/446. Accessed 25 Dec. 2017.

Chua, Amy. *World on Fire: How Free Market Democracy Breeds Ethnic Hatred and Global Instability*. Doubleday, 2003.

Galtung, Johan. "Three Approaches to Peace: Peacekeeping, Peacemaking and Peacebuilding". *Peacebuilding*, edited by Vincent Chetail and Oliver Jütersonke, vol. 1, Routledge, 2015, pp. 13–37.

———. "Twenty-Five Years of Peace Research: Ten Challenges and Some Responses". *Journal of Peace Research*, vol. 22, no. 2, June 1985, pp. 141–158.

He, Yin. "China's Doctrine on UN Peacekeeping". *UN Peacekeeping Doctrine in a New Era*, edited by Cedric de Coning et al., Routledge, 2017, pp. 129–151.

———. "Developmental Peace: Chinese Approach to UN Peacekeeping and Peacebuilding" (fazhan heping: lianheguo weihe jianhe zhong de zhongguo fangan). *The Journal of International Studies* (guoji zhengzhi yanjiu), vol. 38, no. 4, 2017, pp. 10–32.

———. "Norm Competition and Complementation: Peacebuilding as a Case" (guifan jingzheng yu hubu). *The Journal of World Economics and Politics* (shijie jingji yu zhengzhi), no. 4, 2014, pp. 105–121.

———. "United Nations Peacebuilding and the Protection of Human Security" (lianheguo jianshe heping yu rende anquan baohu). *The Journal of International Security* (guoji anquan yanjiu), vol. 32, no. 3, 2014, pp. 75–91.

Ikenberry, G. John. "The Rise of China and the Future of the West: Can the Liberal System Survive?" *Foreign Affairs*, vol. 87, no. 1, Jan.–Feb. 2008, pp. 23–37.

Jenkins, Rob. *Peacebuilding: From Concept to Commission*. Routledge, 2013.

Li, Eric X. "China and the End of Meta-Narratives" (zhongguo jueqi yu yuanxushi de zhongjie). *Chinese Youth* (zhongguo qingnian), no. 11, 2014, pp. 56–57.

Li, Junru. "Be Cautious in Talking 'Chinese Model'" (shenti "zhongguo moshi"). *Communist Party Members Monthly* (gongchandangyuan yuekan), no. 11, 2009, p. 14.

Li, Xing, and Bo Peng. "Rise of China and Transformation of the Global Security Governance" (zhongguo jueqi yu quanqiu anquan zhili zhuanxing). *Journal of International Security* (guoji anquan yanjiu), vol. 34, no. 3, 2016, pp. 51–72.

Lin, Yifu, *New Structural Economics* (xin jiegouzhuyi jingjixue). Beijing UP, 2012.

Mac Ginty, Roger. *International Peacebuilding and Local Resistance: Hybrid Forms of Peace*. Palgrave Macmillan, 2011.

Mac Ginty, Roger, and Oliver Richmond. *The Liberal Peace and Post-War Reconstruction: Myth or Reality?* Routledge, 2009.

Newman, Edward, et al., editors. *New Perspectives on Liberal Peacebuilding*. Edinburgh UP, 2009.

Paris, Roland. "Alternatives to Liberal Peace?" *A Liberal Peace? The Problems and Practices of Peacebuilding*, edited by Susana Campbell et al., Zed Books, 2011, pp. 159–173.

———. *At War's End: Building Peace after Civil Conflict*. Cambridge UP, 2004.

———. "Critiques of Liberal Peace". *A Liberal Peace? The Problems and Practices of Peacebuilding*, edited by Susana Campbell et al., Zed Books, 2011, pp. 31–54.

Reilly, Benjamin. "Elections in Post-Conflict Society". *The UN Role in Promoting Democracy: Between Ideas and Reality*, edited by Edward Newman and Roland Rich, United Nations Press, 2006, pp. 113–134.

Report of the Panel on United Nations Peace Operations. United Nations, 21 Aug. 2000, www.un.org/en/ga/search/view_doc.asp?symbol=A/55/305. Accessed 19 Dec. 2018.

Richmond, Oliver P., and Jason Franks. *Liberal Peace Transitions: Between Statebuilding and Peacebuilding.* Edinburgh UP, 2009.

"Xi Jinping: Pushing for a more Fair and Reasonable Global Governance System" (Xin Jinping: tuidong quanqiu zhili tizhi genjia gongzheng gengjia heli). *Xinhua*, 13 Oct. 2015, www.xinhuanet.com/politics/2015-10/13/c_1116812159.htm. Accessed 20 Dec. 2017.

Zheng, Yongnian. "'Silk Road' and China's Zeitgeist" ("sichou zhilu" yu zhongguo de shidai jingshen). *Huanqiu*, 10 June 2014, http://opinion.huanqiu.com/opinion_world/2014-06/5015986.html. Accessed 28 Dec. 2017.

4 How to curb conflict

Policy lessons from the economic literature

Dominic Rohner[1]

Introduction

While the lion's share of the contributions to this volume on instruments and tools for conflict prevention focus on concrete insights from specific cases and situations, often involving specific policies from China or Switzerland, this chapter takes a step back and offers a survey of statistical results from large-n studies published in economics and political science. Both approaches are useful and complementary, as case studies take particularly well into account concrete and specific features of the context, while an advantage of large-scale statistical studies is that they contain large, well-defined, and comprehensive control groups which allows us to draw general lessons from policies applied elsewhere that may have not received enough attention in other contexts. To give a concrete example, one of the many studies discussed below is about the impact of school construction in Indonesia on the likelihood of political violence (Rohner and Saia). This study finds a very strong pacifying impact from fostering primary education. Obviously these insights cannot be simply blindly applied to other contexts that may be very different from Indonesia. Still, the mechanisms highlighted in this work may well apply beyond Indonesia, and provide inspiration for (maybe smaller scale) pilot projects elsewhere.

Below, I offer a summary of some recent statistical results on peace and war in economics and political science, before highlighting more concretely, towards the end of the essay, how these findings could inspire governments and policy makers. This chapter starts briefly outlining why we should care about tackling turmoil: conflicts are very costly from both a human and socio-economic point of view. After this short discussion of motivation, the emphasis will, second, shift to a few major root causes of fighting, namely poverty, natural resources, and ethnic division. Armed with this overview, the third and final part of this short discussion will then focus on potential medications to cure the ills of political violence.[2]

Costs of conflict

Like the causes, the costs of conflict are manifold, ranging from fatalities over economic costs to societal damage. The maybe most immediate concern and easiest cost to grasp is in terms of human suffering. According to Bae and Ott, the conflict-related deaths in the 20th century were as large as 109.7 million, corresponding to 4.35 percent of the world population. Of these, 60 percent were civilian non-combatants. Hopes that the end of World War II were to give way to a new age of perpetual peace were swiftly dashed: between 1945 and the end of the 20th century, an estimated 3.3 million people lost their lives in 25 interstate wars, while an estimated 16.2 million people perished in 127 civil wars (Fearon and Laitin), and much violence also occurs away from the battlefield, when armed troops turn their weapons against civilians. Since World War II, some 50 episodes of mass killings have led to between 12 and 25 million civilian casualties (Political Instability Task Force).[3]

Also, the economy of a war-torn country gets damaged in various ways. Not only does destruction of physical infrastructure entail a high toll, but also days spent fighting correspond to a loss of productive labor. Unsurprisingly, the economic costs of conflict are sizable by any standard. Collier estimates an average war to reduce annual economic growth by 2.3 percentage points, leading to a total loss of 15 percent of GDP for the average war duration of 7 years. Even conflicts with a below-average death toll, like the separatist fight in Basque Country, can lead to very sizable economic consequences. According to Abadie and Gardeazabal, the comparison of the Basque GDP to a synthetic control group of comparable regions with similar characteristics but without violence, leads to the conclusion that Basque GDP would be about 10% higher today in the absence of ETA's armed fight.

Finally, conflict also imposes costs on the society. While the literature has found a clear-cut effect of conflict exposure during childhood in reducing human capital accumulation (e.g. Shemyakina; Swee) and in increasing future crime propensity (Couttenier et al.), the impact of conflict on social capital is more controversial (see e.g. the survey of Bauer et al.). While some studies have found that conflict depletes trust and boosts ethnic identity (e.g. Cassar et al.; Rohner et al. "Seeds of Distrust"), other studies have also found beneficial effects, in particular on increased local collective action (e.g. Blattman; Bellows and Miguel).

Causes of conflict

Three prominent root causes of political violence have received considerable attention in economics and political science in recent years: poverty, natural resource abundance, and ethnic heterogeneity.

The conceptual reason for the emphasis on poverty as a potential driver of conflict is simple: having a limited amount of time available, people have to choose how to spend it and face an opportunity cost of all options not selected. Concretely, joining a rebel group means giving up work. While the opportunity cost of leaving the work force is low when jobs and perspectives are lacking, it is very high for individuals with large human capital and well-paid jobs. Put differently: it is much easier to recruit fighters in a weak economy. There is indeed a large literature finding that poverty is a powerful correlate of conflict (Fearon and Laitin; Miguel et al.; Collier and Hoeffler; Collier et al.).

A second major factor that has been often investigated as a root cause for conflict is the abundance of natural resources, which represent rents that can be grabbed and a higher price for appropriation. Other mechanisms put forward in the literature include the fact that natural resources may fuel secessionism, that the need of capital for resource extraction may crowd out labor intensive sectors and hence lead to lower wages, or that the control of mines and oil wells makes the financing of rebellion more easily feasible. A variety of articles have documented a strong link between natural resources and conflict, including, among many others, Fearon and Laitin; Collier and Hoeffler; Dube and Vargas; Lei and Michaels; Caselli et al.; Morelli and Rohner; Esteban et al. "Strategic Mass Killings"; and Nicolas Berman et al.

A third often-cited factor is the role of ethnic diversity. One underlying conceptual logic is the idea that ethnicity can be a powerful marker for collective action (see e.g. the theoretical papers of Esteban and Ray; Caselli and Coleman). A variety of statistical studies have found that ethnic polarization goes along with a greater likelihood of civil conflict (Montalvo and Reynal-Querol; Esteban et al. "Ethnicity and Conflict").

Policies for peace

While there is no consensus in the economics of conflict literature on what the key policies are to stop political violence, there are a selection of policies and institutions that appear promising in the light of the empirical evidence. We can group these into four categories: stability; incentives; institutions; and trust.

First, as far as *stability* is concerned, there has been documented the importance of state capacity (Besley and Persson), and in particular the crucial role of establishing security and functioning public service provision (Eli Berman et al.). Second, what has been found to boost *incentives* for peaceful behavior are factors that make the economy strong and that provide jobs and long-run perspectives for prosperity. In particular, education is found to reduce the scope for conflict (Collier and Hoeffler; Thyne; de la Brière et al.; Rohner and Saia), and employment programs and job market access are pointed out as major factors that attenuate the incentives for violent behavior (Blattman and Annan; Couttenier et al.). Related to this are also the findings in Nicolas Berman et al., highlighting that by reducing the potential gains from victorious conflict, peaceful behavior can be promoted. In particular, they find that transparency on mineral origins and high levels of corporate social responsibility attenuate the conflict risk. Third, when it comes to the impact of *institutions*, several articles in the literature have highlighted the non-monotonic impact of democracy. It has been found that regimes with "intermediate" democracy levels face the largest conflict risk (Hegre et al.; Fearon and Laitin), and that democracy tends to reduce conflict in rich countries, while it may fuel conflict in poor states (Collier and Rohner). Two recent studies find a clear impact of full democracy and franchise extension reducing conflict (Laurent-Lucchetti et al.; Rohner and Saia). There exists also evidence for particular aspects of democracy. In particular, institutional constraints, the rule of law, proportional representation, and federalism correlate with having fewer civil wars (Easterly; Reynal-Querol; Saideman et al.; Besley and Persson), and power-sharing has been found to reduce the scope for fighting (Cederman et al.; Mueller and Rohner). Fourth, building *trust* has a variety of angles and aspects. While conceptually it is argued that taking measures that promote inter-group trust may boost inter-group trade and hence increase the opportunity cost of forgone trade in the case of conflict (Rohner et al. "War Signals"), the empirical evidence shows that reconciliation ceremonies (Cilliers et al.) and bilateral pacification of inter-group hostilities can reduce grievances and the scope for conflict (König et al.).

Conclusion

Conflict costs are large by any standards, and directing research efforts at this topic are crucial. While the literature in conflict economics has gained an overview on major causes and consequences of armed fighting, up to recently the study of *how* particular polices can reduce conflict risks has been to a large extent neglected. In recent years, however, a series of interesting results have been reached on how the scope for war can be reduced. Further research on this policy-relevant angle to the conflict question is strongly recommended.

In terms of real-world implications for international policy makers, there are plenty of implications to be drawn in the light of the evidence cited above, in terms of improving stability, incentives, institutions, and trust. To give just one example, education tending in general to be a pacifying force, global policy makers and governments may consider supporting international initiatives and programs – for example, by helping to fund further schooling. But on top of the aforementioned policies that are largely defined at a national level, there are also some inherently transnational policies that may be promising. Nicolas Berman et al. have, for example, found that transparency and certification initiatives for minerals extracted can reduce their potential scope for conflict. This is an example of a cause requiring broad international support and where policy makers and governments around the world can make a real difference through international cooperation.

Notes

1 Dominic Rohner is grateful for helpful comments by Courtney Fung.
2 This current literature review essay draws on earlier survey papers of Rohner ("The Economics of Conflict and Peace"; "The Economics of Peace"). Given its short length, the focus is necessarily selective and the goal is to showcase some relevant recent work on the economics of conflict, without any claim for completeness.
3 Indirect casualties from epidemics and disease among the weakened populations cause at least as many fatalities as direct casualties (Ghobarah et al.). Beyond physical injuries and death, psychological effects of conflict exposure are widely documented (see e.g. Barenbaum et al.).

Bibliography

Abadie, Alberto, and Javier Gardeazabal. "The Economic Costs of Conflict: A Case Study of the Basque Country". *American Economic Review*, vol. 93, no. 1, 2003, pp. 113–132.
Bae, Sang, and Attiat Ott. "Predatory Behavior of Governments: The Case of Mass Killings". *Defence and Peace Economics*, vol. 19, no. 2, 2008, pp. 107–125.
Barenbaum, Joshua, et al. "The Psychosocial Aspects of Children Exposed to War: Practice and Policy Initiatives". *Journal of Child Psychology and Psychiatry*, vol. 45, no. 1, 2004, pp. 41–62.
Bauer, Michal, et al. "Can War Foster Cooperation?" *Journal of Economic Perspectives*, vol. 30, no. 3, 2016, pp. 249–274.

Bellows, John, and Edward Miguel. "War and Local Collective Action in Sierra Leone". *Journal of Public Economics*, vol. 93, no. 11, 2009, pp. 1144–1157.

Berman, Eli, et al. "Can Hearts and Minds Be Bought? The Economics of Counterinsurgency in Iraq". *Journal of Political Economy*, vol. 119, no. 4, 2011, pp. 766–819.

Berman, Nicolas, et al. "This Mine Is Mine! How Minerals Fuel Conflicts in Africa". *American Economic Review*, vol. 107, no. 6, 2017, pp. 1564–1610.

Besley, Timothy, and Torsten Persson. *Pillars of Prosperity*. Princeton UP, 2011.

Blattman, Christopher. "From Violence to Voting: War and Political Participation in Uganda". *American Political Science Review*, vol. 103, no. 2, 2009, pp. 231–247.

Blattman, Christopher, and Jeannie Annan. "Can Employment Reduce Lawlessness and Rebellion? A Field Experiment with High-Risk Men in a Fragile State". *American Political Science Review*, vol. 110, no. 1, 2016, pp. 1–17.

Caselli, Francesco, and Wilbur John Coleman. "On the Theory of Ethnic Conflict". *Journal of the European Economic Association*, vol. 11, no. s1, 2013, pp. 161–192.

Caselli, Francesco, et al. "The Geography of Inter-State Resource Wars". *Quarterly Journal of Economics*, vol. 130, no. 1, 2015, pp. 267–315.

Cassar, Alessandra, et al. "Legacies of Violence: Trust and Market Development". *Journal of Economic Growth*, vol. 18, no. 3, 2013, pp. 285–318.

Cederman, Lars-Erik, et al. *Inequality, Grievances and Civil War*. Cambridge UP, 2013.

Cilliers, Jacobus, et al. "Reconciling after Civil Conflict Increases Social Capital but Decreases Individual Well-Being". *Science*, vol. 352, no. 6287, 2016, pp. 787–794.

Collier, Paul. *The Bottom Billion: Why the Poorest Countries Are Failing and What Can Be Done About It*. Oxford UP, 2007.

Collier, Paul, and Anke Hoeffler. "Greed and Grievance in Civil War". *Oxford Economic Papers*, vol. 56, no. 4, 2004, pp. 563–595.

Collier, Paul, et al. "Beyond Greed and Grievance: Feasibility and Civil War". *Oxford Economic Papers*, vol. 61, no. 1, 2009, pp. 1–27.

Collier, Paul, and Dominic Rohner. "Democracy, Development, and Conflict". *Journal of the European Economic Association*, vol. 6, no. 2–3, 2008, pp. 531–540.

Couttenier, Mathieu, et al. "The Violent Legacy of Victimization: Post-Conflict Evidence on Asylum Seekers, Crimes and Public Policy in Switzerland". *CEPR Discussion Papers*, no. 11079, U of Geneva and U of Lausanne, 2018.

de la Brière, Bénédicte, et al. *From Mines and Wells to Well-Built Minds: Turning Sub-Saharan Africa's Natural Resource Wealth Into Human Capital*. World Bank, 2017.

Dube, Oeindrila, and Juan F. Vargas. "Commodity Price Shocks and Civil Conflict: Evidence from Colombia". *The Review of Economic Studies*, vol. 80, no. 4, 2013, pp. 1384–1421.

Easterly, William. "Can Institutions Resolve Ethnic Conflict?" *Economic Development and Cultural Change*, vol. 49, no. 4, 2001, pp. 687–706.

Esteban, Joan, et al. "Ethnicity and Conflict: An Empirical Study". *American Economic Review*, vol. 102, no. 4, 2012, pp. 1310–1342.

Esteban, Joan, et al. "Strategic Mass Killings". *Journal of Political Economy*, vol. 123, no. 5, 2015, pp. 1087–1132.

Esteban, Joan, and Debraj Ray. "On the Salience of Ethnic Conflict". *American Economic Review*, vol. 98, no. 5, 2008, pp. 2185–2202.

Fearon, James, and David Laitin. "Ethnicity, Insurgency, and Civil War". *American Political Science Review*, vol. 97, no. 1, 2003, pp. 75–90.

Ghobarah, Hazem Adam, et al. "Civil Wars Kill and Maim People – Long After the Shooting Stops". *American Political Science Review*, vol. 97, no. 2, 2003, pp. 189–202.

Hegre, Håvard, et al. "Toward a Democratic Civil Peace? Democracy, Political Change, and Civil War, 1816–1992". *The American Political Science Review*, vol. 95, no. 1, 2001, pp. 33–48.

König, Michael D., et al. "Networks in Conflict: Theory and Evidence from the Great War of Africa". *Econometrica*, vol. 85, no. 4, 2017, pp. 1093–1132.

Laurent-Lucchetti, Jeremy, Dominic Rohner, and Mathias Thoenig. "Ethnic Conflicts and the Informational Dividend of Democracy". Working Paper, 2020.

Lei, Yu-Hsiang, and Guy Michaels. "Do Giant Oilfield Discoveries Fuel Internal Armed Conflicts?" *Journal of Development Economics*, vol. 110(C), 2014, pp. 139–157.

Miguel, Edward, et al. "Economic Shocks and Civil Conflict: An Instrumental Variables Approach". *Journal of Political Economy*, vol. 112, no. 4, 2004, pp. 725–753.

Montalvo, José G., and Marta Reynal-Querol. "Ethnic Polarization, Potential Conflict, and Civil Wars". *The American Economic Review*, vol. 95, no. 3, 2005, pp. 796–816.

Morelli, Massimo, and Dominic Rohner. "Resource Concentration and Civil Wars". *Journal of Development Economics*, vol. 117, 2015, pp. 32–47.

Mueller, Hannes, and Dominic Rohner. "Can Power-Sharing Foster Peace? Evidence from Northern Ireland". *Economic Policy*, vol. 33, no. 95, 2018, pp. 447–484.

Political Instability Task Force. "Genocides". *Dataset*. https://scip.gmu.edu/political-instability-task-force/.

Reynal-Querol, Marta. "Ethnicity, Political Systems, and Civil Wars". *Journal of Conflict Resolution*, vol. 46, no. 1, 2002, pp. 29–54.

Rohner, Dominic. "The Economics of Conflict and Peace". *Emerging Trends in the Social and Behavioral Science*, edited by R. A. Scott and S. M. Kosslyn, Wiley, 2017.

Rohner, Dominic, and Alessandro Saia. "Ballot or Bullet: The Impact of UK's Representation of the People Act on Peace and Prosperity". Working Paper, 2020.

———. "The Economics of Peace: Can 'Swiss' Institutions Do the Job?" *Public Policy Papers*, UBS International Center of Economics in Society at the U of Zurich, 2016.

Rohner, Dominic, and Alessandro Saia. "Education and Conflict: Evidence from a Policy Experiment in Indonesia". *CEPR Discussion Papers*, no. 13509, U of Lausanne, 2018.

Rohner, Dominic, et al. "Seeds of Distrust: Conflict in Uganda". *Journal of Economic Growth*, vol. 18, no. 3, 2013, pp. 217–252.

———. "War Signals: A Theory of Trade, Trust, and Conflict". *The Review of Economic Studies*, vol. 80, no. 3, 2013, pp. 1114–1147, doi:10.1093/restud/rdt003.

Saideman, Stephen M., et al. "Democratization, Political Institutions, and Ethnic Conflict: A Pooled Time-Series Analysis, 1985–1998". *Comparative Political Studies*, vol. 35, no. 1, 2002, pp. 103–129.

Shemyakina, Olga. "The Effect of Armed Conflict on Accumulation of Schooling: Results from Tajikistan". *Journal of Development Economics*, vol. 95, no. 2, 2011, pp. 186–200.

Swee, Eik Leong. "On War Intensity and Schooling Attainment: The Case of Bosnia and Herzegovina". *European Journal of Political Economy*, vol. 40, 2015, pp. 158–172.

Thyne, Clayton L. "ABC's, 123's, and the Golden Rule: The Pacifying Effect of Education on Civil War, 1980–1999". *International Studies Quarterly*, vol. 50, no. 4, 2006, pp. 733–754.

Part II
Approaches to preventing conflict

5 The deep roots of Swiss conflict prevention

David Lanz

Introduction

Switzerland is known as a neutral country with an active peace policy. The Swiss themselves consider conflict prevention an essential feature of foreign affairs, and, indeed, peace promotion is enshrined in the Swiss constitution as one of five objectives of its external relations. Internally, Switzerland's political system is underpinned by the need to manage diversity in a heterogeneous society, accommodating people speaking different languages, practicing different religions, and having different socio-economic backgrounds, in order to ensure peaceful coexistence.

How to explain Switzerland's focus on conflict prevention? What are the deep roots of Switzerland's internal and external conflict prevention efforts? How does Switzerland prevent conflict? This essay explores these questions by first outlining Switzerland's geopolitical profile, taking into account its geography, economy, demography, and political history. It then surveys Swiss infrastructures for the prevention of internal conflict and finally looks at the country's policy on preventing conflicts abroad.

Geopolitical profile of Switzerland

What are the main features of Switzerland's geopolitical profile? A glimpse at the world map reveals that Switzerland is a relatively small, landlocked country located in the middle of Western Europe. With the exception of Liechtenstein, Switzerland's neighbors, i.e. Germany, France, Italy, and Austria, are larger countries and count among Europe's great powers that have shaped the turbulent history of the continent. While the Alps mountain range covers about 60%

of Switzerland's territory, over two thirds of its 8 million inhabitants live on the plateau north of the Alps with few natural boundaries vis-à-vis neighboring countries. Historically speaking, the implication of Switzerland's small-state status is that the country could not primarily rely on military defense for its survival. In times when the use of force, and the conquest of one state's territory by another state, was common, a policy of neutrality emerged as the best approach for Switzerland to avoid being drawn into military confrontations with or between large powers. Therefore, its small-state geography implies that Switzerland has an existential interest in a peaceful world order and, in particular, in good relations among European powers.

Concerning the economy, Switzerland's small size implies that its internal market is limited. This means that the development of an export industry and opportunities to trade with other countries were crucial to generate wealth. Looking at Switzerland's economic history, it was indeed in the second half of the 19th century when growth rates shot up thanks to companies producing goods and services for the export market (Bergier). In essence, Switzerland's economic outward orientation meant that the country depended on a peaceful world order, where conflicts are contained and prevented, both for its security and for its welfare.

Switzerland's demographic makeup reveals a heterogeneous society with linguistic diversity, German, French, Italian, and Romansch being official national languages, as well as religious diversity, as the country is divided between Catholics and Protestants. Politically, Switzerland functioned as a confederacy until the mid-19th century: an alliance of territories that worked together in some areas, but remained politically independent. In 1848, following a short civil war, Switzerland became a federal state. Some power was pooled in the center, although the constituent parts, the cantons, remained strong (Maissen). Switzerland thus never had a central authority to impose order and, likewise, the heterogeneous nature of Swiss society meant that no dominant way of life emerged, assimilating other cultures. To hold the country together, Switzerland had to find ways to manage its diversity and prevent conflict. The country therefore needed to develop mechanisms for different groups to negotiate with each other and resolve their differences, thus ensuring peaceful coexistence.

In sum, this essay argues that Switzerland's geopolitical profile – its geography, economy, demography, and political history – explains why conflict prevention is an existential interest, internally to maintain the unity of the country and externally to ensure security and welfare. The two subsequent sections deepen the internal and external dimensions, focusing on mechanisms that put Swiss conflict prevention into practice.

Mechanisms for conflict prevention within Switzerland

After the establishment of the federal state in 1848, Switzerland progressively developed an infrastructure to prevent conflicts from emerging and, when tensions did arise, to prevent them from escalating. The most important institution in this regard is federalism: the idea that power is shared between constituent parts and the center, where the constituent parts are also represented. Modeled after the US system, Switzerland features 26 cantons (including six so-called half-cantons), which have their own constitution and possess a high degree of autonomy in many fields, including taxes, education, courts, and police. At the federal level, the Swiss parliament, the Federal Assembly, consists of two chambers: the National Council, with proportional representation based on population size, and the Council of States, where each canton has two seats (except for half-cantons, which have one seat each) (Vatter). The core idea behind federalism is subsidiarity: decisions are taken where people are directly affected by them. This reduces conflict vis-à-vis the center and between different regions of the country, allowing them to preserve their identities and political cultures (Fleiner et al.).

A second conflict prevention mechanism is called "concordance" (*Konkordanz* in German). This refers to a political system predicated on consensus and compromise, where relevant stakeholders are involved, and their interests taken into account, before a decision is taken. One aspect of concordance pertains to the composition of the Swiss national government, i.e. the Federal Council, which includes seven members from the major parties and regions. The bicameral parliamentary system means that the interests of cantons are taken into account in the law-making process. Moreover, the parliament practices an institutionalized multi-stakeholder consultation process (*Vernehmlassung* in German), in which all interest groups concerning a specific policy area are heard (Iff and Töpperwien 29–36).

What happens when there is a conflict? Courts play a certain role. For example, the Federal Supreme Court decides in matters where there is a conflict between the federal constitution and the constitution of a canton. However, the role of courts is relatively limited in the Swiss political system. For example, there is no constitutional review, allowing the Federal Supreme Court to invalidate a law adopted by the national parliament on the grounds of its inconsistency with the federal constitution (Iff and Töpperwien 56–62). The more common, and more accepted, conflict resolution mechanism in Switzerland involves votes and referenda. If 50,000 Swiss citizens sign a petition opposing a bill adopted by parliament, a nationwide referendum will be held to take the final decision. 100,000 signatures will bring an initiative for a constitutional amendment to a vote. Finally, if the federal government or the parliament wants to change the constitution, a nationwide vote automatically takes place to decide on the matter. Decisions adopted in nationwide votes have a high degree of legitimacy and are more easily accepted by losers, thus preventing polarization and conflict (Linder). Further reducing conflict in Switzerland is a well-functioning rule of law, as well as the rights and freedoms enjoyed by citizens. As a result, there has been a low level of internal conflict since the establishment of the federal state in 1848, even if the compromise orientation of the political system means that decision-making is slower than in other countries.

One example to illustrate Swiss internal conflict prevention pertains to the conflict in Jura, a French-speaking and Catholic region that was part of the predominantly German-speaking and Protestant Canton of Bern. A separatist movement emerged in the 1950s, demanding autonomy for the "Jurassic" people and decrying Bern's cultural and political domination. Throughout the 1960s, the movement grew more militant and committed acts of sabotage, provoking a forceful response by the Bernese police (Bassand). As it became apparent that the creation of a new canton in Jura had widespread support and as the government of the Canton of Bern feared losing control, a series of votes were held to address the problem and eventually defuse the situation. In 1970, a vote was held in the entire territory of the canton about whether or not to amend the constitution allowing for a part of its territory to separate and establish a new canton. The vote was affirmative, albeit with a small margin. Subsequently, in 1974, a vote took place in all municipalities of the Jura asking inhabitants whether they wanted to establish a new canton. The result was again affirmative. One year later, in 1975, another vote took place in the same municipalities, asking people whether they wanted to join a new canton of Jura or remain with Bern. Areas with a majority of French speakers voted to join the new canton, whereas areas with a majority of German speakers voted to remain with Bern, leading to a contiguous territory for the new canton. Finally, a nationwide vote took place in 1978 approving a change of the

Swiss constitution allowing for the creation of a new canton with all rights and privileges. Given the affirmative outcome, in January 1979, Jura became the 26th canton of Switzerland, and tensions subsequently diminished.[1]

Switzerland's efforts to prevent conflicts abroad

What does conflict prevention mean for Switzerland's external relations? The cornerstone of Swiss foreign policy is neutrality. It derived from a desire to avoid being drawn into great-power conflict, an essential survival strategy practiced by Switzerland as well as other small states. There is an internal dimension of neutrality too: given the heterogeneity of Swiss society, siding with one or the other side in conflicts could have led to split loyalties and jeopardized the cohesion of the country. The origins of neutrality go back to 1515 when the Swiss Confederacy lost to France in the Battle of Marignano, although it was only formalized in 1815 when the European powers at the Vienna Congress stipulated Switzerland's "perpetual neutrality" (Goetschel et al.).

What does neutrality mean and how is it connected to conflict prevention? The legal core of neutrality refers to the duty to abstain from supporting warring parties, coupled with the right of having its territorial integrity respected.[2] However, neutrality does not dictate a specific foreign policy and indeed, debates about what type of external engagement neutrality mandates are prevalent and recurring (Rhinow). Since 1848, Switzerland has vacillated between more isolationist and more active interpretations of neutrality. Actions to prevent conflict abroad are part of a more active foreign policy based on the idea that neutrality is a reputational asset that gives Switzerland credibility to promote a peaceful world order. This explains why actions to promote peace and prevent conflict are, as today, a central component of Swiss foreign policy during certain periods, but more marginal in others.

Active peace-promotion efforts started in the second half of the 19th century after the establishment of the federal state when a national foreign policy took shape. For example, Switzerland took over protective power mandates, representing countries vis-à-vis others with whom diplomatic relations were ruptured. It also hosted international conferences and organizations, for example, a conference in Geneva in 1864, at which states adopted the First Geneva Convention, the founding act of international humanitarian law. Switzerland also hosted arbitration tribunals, including the first such tribunal dealing with claims made by the United States against the United Kingdom for its involvement in the American Civil War from 1861 to 1865, which had poisoned the relations between the two countries and led to threats of war. After the Second World War, Switzerland took a more isolationist stance and refrained from joining the United Nations in 1945. However, during the Cold War, Switzerland engaged in some bridge-building activities. It maintained good relations with countries in the socialist block and, in 1950, was one of the first Western countries to recognize the People's Republic of China. Examples of conflict prevention during the Cold War include the involvement of the Swiss military in the Nations Supervisory Commission in Korea of 1953, an engagement that continues until today. Other examples are the protective power mandate related to US–Cuba relations, Switzerland's active diplomatic role in the establishment of the Conference on Security and Cooperation in Europe, and hosting the Gorbachev–Reagan meeting in 1985.[3]

After the end of the Cold War, peace promotion was elevated to one of the core pillars of Swiss foreign policy and enshrined in the Swiss constitution.[4] While Switzerland's engagement in military peacekeeping has remained limited, civilian peacebuilding expanded. A federal law on civilian peace promotion was adopted in 2002, and Switzerland became a member of the UN in the same year. Within the Federal Department of Foreign Affairs (FDFA), a specific division with a funding line from parliament was created under the banner of "Human Security", implementing a broad range of measures, ranging from mediation, dealing with the past, humanitarian policy, and human rights.[5] Support for conflict prevention also increased in the Swiss population. For example, a representative survey in 2013 showed that over 90% of Swiss citizens find it "important or very important" that their country engages in international peace promotion (swisspeace).

The result is that in the past 15 years, Switzerland has taken an active role in preventing conflicts in different parts of the world. One example is Nepal, where Switzerland helped facilitate a comprehensive peace agreement in 2006, preventing an escalation of violence and paving the way for a political transition that ended a ten-year civil war (Bächler). Likewise, in Sudan, Switzerland provided political and technical support in the negotiations that led to the Comprehensive Peace Agreement of 2005 (Greminger). A more recent example, acting through a multilateral organization, is Switzerland's chairmanship of the Organization for Security and Cooperation in Europe (OSCE) in 2014. Under the leadership of Switzerland, the OSCE responded swiftly to the Ukraine crisis, setting up a monitoring mission as well as a format for political negotiations. Both mechanisms have helped to curb violence escalation, even if they have not resolved the conflict (Nünlist).

Conclusion

Two concluding insights derive from Switzerland's experience in conflict prevention. The first pertains to the deep roots of conflict prevention anchored in Switzerland's geopolitical disposition as a small state with a federal structure and a heterogeneous society. Conflict prevention, therefore, represents a fundamental interest for Switzerland. Over time, it has become part of national identity, as many citizens consider conflict prevention a core value to be upheld inside the country and to be promoted internationally.

Second, conflict prevention mechanisms did not automatically emerge, but were the outcome of negotiations, and re-negotiations, between different groups throughout Swiss history. This means that the specific mechanisms used in Switzerland for conflict prevention are tailored to the specific national context and as such, they are not one-to-one transferrable to other countries. For example, holding popular votes works in Switzerland because they are embedded in a compromise-based political culture. In the absence of this, popular votes risk dividing the populace and fueling conflict, rather than preventing it. However, there are aspects of the Swiss experience in conflict prevention – for example, managing diversity in society through a multi-layered system of power-sharing – that do offer relevant lessons for other countries.

Notes

1 While the creation of the Canton of Jura resolved the situation overall, tensions continued to simmer in some areas, in particular the municipality of Moutier, which is divided nearly 50:50 between German and French speakers. In 1975, Moutier, by a small margin, voted to remain with Bern. Because of continued tensions, another vote was held in Moutier in June 2017, and this time, again by a narrow margin, a majority voted to join the canton of Jura. However, the vote was declared invalid in November 2018 and thus the final outcome remains unclear.
2 On the legal aspects of neutrality, see a background file prepared by the International Committee of the Red Cross.
3 On the evolution of Swiss peace policy, see Graf and Lanz.
4 Article 54, paragraph 2, of the Swiss Constitution as amended in 1999 stipulates:

The Confederation shall ensure that the independence of Switzerland and its welfare is safeguarded; it shall in particular assist in the alleviation of need and poverty in the world and promote respect for human rights and democracy, the peaceful co-existence of peoples as well as the conservation of natural resources.

5   For details, see website of the FDFA Human Security Division.

Bibliography

Activating Democracy. "The Jura Conflict: Direct Democracy in Action". www. activatingdemocracy.com/topics/stories/the-jura-conflict-direct-democracy-in-practice/. Accessed 10 June 2018.

Bächler, Günther. "Adapt Facilitation to Changing Contexts". *Swiss Peace Policy: Nepal*, edited by Swiss FDFA, 2008, pp. 14–50.

Bassand, Michel. "The Jura Problem". *Journal of Peace Research*, vol. 12, no. 2, 1975, pp. 139–150.

Bergier, Jean-François. *Histoire économique de la Suisse*. Armand Colin, 1984.

Federal Department of Foreign Affairs FDFA. "Human Security Division". FDFA, 15 Jan. 2018 www.fdfa.admin.ch/eda/en/home/fdfa/organisation-fdfa/directorates-divisions/directorate-political-affairs/hsd.html. Accessed 10 June 2018.

Fleiner, Thomas, et al. "Federalism, Decentralization and Conflict Management in Multicultural Societies". *Politorbis*, vol. 32, no. 1, 2003, pp. 39–57.

Goetschel, Laurent, et al. *Swiss Foreign Policy: Foundations and Possibilities*. Routledge, 2005.

Graf, Andreas, and David Lanz. "Conclusions: Switzerland as a Paradigmatic Case of Small-State Peace Policy?" *Swiss Political Science Review*, vol. 19, no. 3, 2013, pp. 410–423.

Greminger, Thomas. *Swiss Civilian Peace Promotion: Assessing Policy and Practice*. Zurich, Center for Security Studies & ETH, 2011.

Iff, Andrea, and Nicole Töpperwien. "Power-Sharing: the Swiss Experience". *Politorbis*, vol. 45, no. 2, 2008.

International Committee of the Red Cross. "The Law of Armed Conflict: Neutrality". ICRC, 2002. www.icrc.org/eng/assets/files/other/law8_final.pdf; www.icrc.org/eng/assets/files/other/law8_final.pdf.

Linder, Wolf. "Direkte Demokratie". *Handbuch der Schweizer Politik*, edited by Peter Knoepfel et al., 5th ed., NZZ Libro, 2014, pp. 145–168.

Maissen, Thomas. *Geschichte der Schweiz*. Verlag Hier und Jetzt, 2012.

Nünlist, Christian. "Testfall Ukraine-Krise: Das Konfliktmanagement der OSZE unter Schweizer Vorsitz". *Bulletin 2014 zur schweizerischen Sicherheitspolitik*, Center for Security Studies, 2014, pp. 35–61.

Rhinow, René. "Neutralität als Deckmantel für eine aktive oder Restriktive Aussenpolitik". *Die Schweizer Neutralität*, edited by G. Kreis, Werd Verlag, 2007, pp. 19–35.

swisspeace. "Schweizer Friedensförderung geniesst sehr hohen Stellenwert bei der Bevölkerung". www.swisspeace.ch/fileadmin/user_upload/Media/etc/Media/Media_Releases/2013_Umfrage_def_1Juli2013.pdf. Accessed 10 June 2018.

Vatter, Adrian. "Föderalismus". *Handbuch der Schweizer Politik*, edited by Peter Knoepfel et al., 5th ed., NZZ Libro, 2014, pp. 119–144.

6 Considerations for the design and preparation of national dialogue processes

Katia Papagianni

Introduction

National dialogues are negotiating mechanisms designed to include several constituencies during political transitions or post-conflict periods. In some contemporary conflict settings, the traditional peacemaking approach of negotiations among a few leaders representing clearly defined interest groups may be unable to accommodate the diversity of conflict parties. Such conflicts include situations where multiple armed groups are active, state institutions have fragmented, or incumbent regimes are being challenged and oppositions not well-organized. It is therefore sensible to design peace processes that seek to accommodate the diversity of actors.[1]

National dialogues usually include a minimum of a couple of hundred people and bring together diverse constituencies, such as political parties, armed groups, militia, members of government and parliament, civil society organizations, professional associations, religious institutions and leaders, tribal leaders, and prominent citizens. The defining characteristics of a national dialogue are: large; inclusive of various constituencies; addressing multiple national issues; and mandated to offer recommendations and in some cases take decisions.

The ambition of national dialogue is to move away from elite-level negotiations by allowing diverse interests to participate. National dialogues are not purely democratic processes: their participants are not chosen through direct one-man-one-vote elections but are either appointed or selected by caucus-type constituencies that are smaller than the total population of voting age. Also, national dialogue processes design their own debating and decision-making rules. National dialogues try to escape the elitism of peace negotiations, but do not provide for a full-fledged democratic process.

There are three inherent tensions in designing national dialogue processes, which influence their legitimacy and effectiveness. The first tension relates to their size and composition. How large should national dialogues be? What constituencies need to be included and how should their representatives be selected? A second tension relates to the power and mandate of national dialogues. What is their relationship to existing state institutions like parliaments and governments? Finally, a third tension inherent in national dialogues, and related to the second one, is the question of their independence. Should the decisions of national dialogues be ratified by existing institutions or should their decisions be final? These tensions are usually resolved through negotiations among the key political actors. These negotiations are by definition messy and difficult. Often, key political actors agree on a set of principles that should govern the transition, which they then seek to consolidate through an inclusive national dialogue. In other cases, the above tensions are resolved during the dialogue process itself, while in yet others they lead to the failure of the dialogue.

The preparatory process

The preparation of a national dialogue process can often be lengthy and is central to its success. Typically, a widely representative committee is established with the responsibility to prepare all aspects of the dialogue. The appointment of the preparatory committee can be highly contested and often results from extensive negotiations. The composition of such a committee and the process through which it is negotiated influences whether it is accepted as legitimate by the various political forces.

Once in place, the work of the preparatory committee is itself a negotiation process which can be lengthy and can lead to an agreement on a clear mandate for the dialogue, if such an agreement is not already in place. Typically, the preparatory committee is responsible for: defining the criteria for participation in the dialogue and the process through which the participants will be selected; supervising the selection process; drafting the outline of the dialogue agenda; establishing a support structure for the duration of the dialogue, usually in the form of a secretariat; and preparing all the administrative and logistics aspects of the dialogue including venue, security, and other aspects.

In Yemen, a 25-member Technical Committee (TC) was established by Presidential Decree in July 2012 and worked for more than six months. The TC had the mandate to prepare all aspects of the National Dialogue Conference (NDC) but "in no way anticipate or prejudice the substantive work and outcomes of the Conference".[2] The November 2011 Implementation Mechanism had defined the constituencies to be represented in the NDC, which were also included in the TC. These constituencies included the political parties which signed the 2011 agreement that ended the conflict as well as the other constituencies listed in the agreement, including the Houthi Movement, youth, civil society, and women. The TC was boycotted by the Southern Movement (a political movement with secessionist elements in the Southern part of the country), although some persons linked to it agreed to join the TC.

The TC worked until February 2013 and published a detailed report which included records of its discussions on the key issues related to the preparation of the NDC.[3] The most important products of the TC's work were the Rules of Procedure for the NDC, which included the NDC's decision-making procedures and the relationship between the NDC's plenary and its working groups. The TC also decided the division of the NDC's 565 seats among the various constituencies. These decisions consumed several months of negotiation.

In Benin, president Kerekou appointed a diverse preparatory committee to decide the conference's agenda and composition. The committee identified the groups which would be allowed to participate in the conference, and specified how many representatives they would each be allotted. Subsequently, each group chose their own delegates. The 500-member conference included both representatives of the government and the military as well as Kerekou's enemies in political exile (Heilbrunn 286). It also included representatives of all trade unions, religious leaders, voluntary associations, women's groups, several former heads of state, and a variety of public figures (Nwajiaku 429; Wiseman 86).

In Niger, in 1991, a 68-member preparatory commission was established in order to decide the mandate and composition of the national conference. The composition of both the preparatory commission and the national conference were debated extensively. The 1,204 delegates to the national conference represented political parties, trade unions, professional groups, and civic associations. Both the conference and its elected presidium included many members of the trade unions and the student movement ("Niger National Conference Postponed"; "Niger Further Details"; Gervais 93–94). In Mali, the conference was appointed by the transitional government and was attended by 1,800 delegates including representatives of the newly created political parties, religious groups, trade unions, women's groups, students, and peasant representatives (Wiseman 88).

The selection of participants

Given that the goal of political dialogues is to generate society-wide consensus on major reforms that a country needs to adopt, it is important that as many political, military, and social groups as possible are included in the dialogue. Most political dialogues include the main political parties, armed groups, and civil society organizations. In some cases, professional associations and state institutions are also included. Most dialogues ensure the representation of women, youth, and marginalized groups.

The following are some considerations in deciding the composition of a political dialogue:

- What groups have sizable constituencies and can claim to be the legitimate representatives of these constituencies?
- What groups have the power to influence the implementation of any decisions the political dialogue may take?
- What groups have a track record of working in an impartial and non-partisan manner to solve some of the country's problems?
- What groups have creative ideas on how to solve the country's problems?
- What groups have expertise and knowledge on the issues discussed by the dialogue?

Based on the above considerations, a combination of political, military, state, and civil society actors is likely to generate a wide consensus. In order to achieve this representation, political dialogues often reserve a sizable number of seats for independents, civil society actors, expert professionals, women, and youth.

The method adopted for selecting the participants of national dialogues is closely scrutinized by social and political actors. In the absence of direct elections where every adult has the right to cast a vote, designing a representative, legitimate, and efficient selection process is difficult. Also, questions inevitably arise about the authority and legitimacy of those developing the selection method. Ultimately, the composition of national dialogues has resulted from lengthy negotiations among the key political forces.

The selection method for the dialogue participants is usually developed through a several-step process, which is typically contentious. First, a political agreement is reached, often through the work of the preparatory body, on the constituencies which are to be included in the dialogue. These constituencies might include political parties, civil society, regions, religious leaders, ethnic groups, minorities, and professional associations. Identifying the constituencies may be straightforward in some countries where the main social and political groups are clear. In other cases, though, introducing certain groups as constituencies with the right to be represented can be contentious. In Yemen, for example, some argued that independent youth, women, and civil society were not separate constituencies but should rather be subsumed under political parties. However, these three groups were listed in the 2011 peace agreement and ultimately it proved difficult to prevent them from participating in the dialogue as separate constituencies.

As a second step, the preparatory body agrees on the sub-categories belonging to each constituency. For example, a number of decisions need to be taken on how to sub-divide the constituency of "political parties": does it include only parliamentary parties or also extra-parliamentary parties, does it include older parties or also newly established ones? In Iraq, the debate over the representation of political parties in the national conference was vigorous. Out of the estimated 1,200–1,400 participants in the Conference, 144 seats were given to political party representatives according to a formula which placed parties in three categories based on the number of years since their establishment. The oldest parties received six delegates, the other categories three and one. This was understandably disputed. Leaders of new parties argued that, in the absence of elections, it was impossible to evaluate party strength and that the criterion was arbitrary. Furthermore, choosing which of the more than 150 Iraqi parties to include was a formidable challenge (Papagianni "National Conferences in Transitional Periods" 326).

The third step in determining the composition of a dialogue process is to decide its size. In some cases, political actors prefer large dialogues of several thousand persons. In general, such large dialogues tend to have few decision-making powers as it is difficult to discuss in detail the key issues facing a country within a gathering of thousands of persons. In other cases, political actors propose very small dialogues of 100 or 200 persons in order to ensure that they engage in detailed discussions, including on constitutional principles. This option usually makes it difficult for the dialogue to be inclusive and to serve as a negotiation vehicle that differs from the elite-dominated negotiations. The size of the dialogue then is a balance between the needs imposed by inclusion and efficiency.

The fourth step in selecting the participants is to design the actual selection methodology of the dialogue participants. There are several methodologies to be considered which may be grouped under three categories:

1. Appointment of the dialogue participants by the preparatory body and/or the executive or parliament of the country (in cases where they are involved in the process).
2. Self-selection by the identified constituencies of their representatives to the dialogue.
3. Regional/local selection processes through caucus-type gatherings.

In some cases two or even three of the above were combined. The difficulties with the first approach are linked to legitimacy. Even if the preparatory body is well-respected, appointing the dialogue participants might be perceived as over-stepping its powers. The second approach of self-selection by the constituencies themselves carries the benefit of real representation for the chosen constituencies. Constituencies which are well organized may be able to agree on their representatives to the dialogue relatively easily. However, the approach does not work well in the case of divided constituencies or of constituencies which are not well-organized. Constituencies such as "civil society", "women", "religious leaders", or "regions" may not be able to easily agree on their representatives. In these cases, the risk is that one faction or a handful of individuals select the representatives for the whole constituency.

The delegates to the 2004 Iraqi national conference were chosen through two selection processes. About 548 of the delegates were selected through a provincial process designed by the High Preparatory Committee (HPC), while the rest were appointed by the HPC. In each of Iraq's 18 provinces, the HPC appointed a provincial committee responsible for selecting the participants of a provincial meeting, which elected the province's delegates to the conference. Persons interested in participating in the provincial meeting submitted applications to the committee. Each provincial meeting consisted of 20 times more persons than the number of delegates elected by that province. Twenty-five percent of the delegates of each province had to be women. The committees had three to four days to carry out their task: one or two days to inform the public and receive applications to attend the meeting, and a similar time for deliberations and choosing participants (Papagianni "National Conferences in Transitional Periods" 325–326).

The rest of the Iraqi national conference delegates were appointed by the HPC, whose 100 members automatically got seats in the conference. Initially another 360 national, appointed delegates were planned, of whom 144 would be members of political parties, 72 representatives of civic organizations, 70 tribal leaders, and 74 other personalities.

The mandate

National dialogues benefit from a clear and manageable mandate, and a well-defined relationship to ongoing political processes which is negotiated prior to the commencement of the dialogue. The mandate is usually negotiated among key political, social, and military actors and endorsed by the relevant existing state institutions. These negotiations and endorsements ensure that major actors are committed to the dialogue and agree on the goals of the dialogue. This strengthens the legitimacy of the dialogue and reduces the possibility of disagreement, once the dialogue commences, regarding its goals and powers.

In cases where negotiation among all major groups and endorsement by the widest possible number of actors and institutions does not occur, there is a risk that some groups refuse to participate in the dialogue or may actively undermine it.

Those responsible for preparing political dialogues negotiate the following questions:

- What will the dialogue discuss?
  It is important that the list of issues to be discussed by the dialogue is manageable and not over-ambitious. A long list of issues may lead to some of them not being properly discussed.
- What powers will the dialogue have?
  A political dialogue may have the power to provide recommendations which other existing institutions (e.g. parliament or government) can adopt or reject. Alternatively, the dialogue may take decisions which other institutions are required to accept. A hybrid model would give a political dialogue strong decision-making powers, but would also give other institutions the authority to discuss the dialogue's decisions before endorsing them.
- How will the dialogue relate to existing institutions?
  National political dialogues usually do not formally report to existing state institutions during their deliberations. However, in some cases, representatives of the government or parliament participate in the dialogue. This allows these institutions to follow developments within the dialogue and may encourage them to implement the dialogue's decisions.
- How long will the dialogue last?
  Given that national political dialogues attempt to address contentious and complex issues, they need enough time to discuss everything on their agenda, negotiate the needed reforms, and reach agreements. At the same time, dialogue processes may lose momentum and direction, if they last too long. Therefore, those who design and prepare political dialogues need to agree on a duration which allows for adequate deliberation without risking losing momentum, direction, and attention by leaders and public.

The working method

Most dialogues tend to divide their work between plenary meetings and working groups. Given that the plenary may include several hundred participants, in-depth discussion tends to take place in working groups. As a result, most of the substantive work of a political dialogue may take place in working groups.

This means that working groups need to be carefully designed and usually follow a set of considerations:

- Working groups usually have balanced representation in order to ensure that their proposals are accepted by all constituencies participating in the dialogue.
- Working groups have clear rules of procedure in order to ensure that they function efficiently and effectively.
- Political dialogues benefit from clear rules outlining the relationship between the plenary and the working groups.
- Political dialogues usefully rely upon a mechanism which facilitates regular communication among the various working groups and ensures that most participants are aware of developments in most working groups.
- National dialogues benefit from a mechanism which tracks developments in the various working groups and ensures the cohesion of the dialogue's proceedings.
- Political dialogues benefit from a conflict resolution mechanism which assists the members of working groups to overcome disputes and reach agreements.

Political dialogues which last a few months tend to meet a few times in plenary form, while their working groups may meet daily for extensive periods of time and reconvene after short breaks. In general, political dialogues tend to meet and work intensively.

Planning and support

The preparation of political dialogues is a highly political and contentious process. The question of who contributes to the preparation of the dialogue is contentious and may influence the legitimacy of the dialogue. There are usually three considerations regarding the participants of the preparatory process:

- The preparations of a national dialogue benefit from the active participation and support of the leaders of all key constituencies. High-level support of the preparations ensures that the decisions of the preparatory process will be implemented.
- Ideally, all relevant constituencies should participate in the preparations of the political dialogue. This ensures that the decisions taken are perceived as legitimate by most constituencies.
- The preparations benefit from technical and expert support which may not be available among those responsible for the preparations.

National dialogues are complex events and require detailed administrative preparations and logistical planning. These preparations can be contentious and political. For example, the selection of the venue(s) for the dialogue is often not only a logistical task, but also a political one due to security and symbolic considerations. Also, the establishment of administrative and expert support structures for a political dialogue can be a political task as the constituencies participating in the dialogue may wish to influence these structures. It is therefore advisable that the administrative planning is given great attention and, if possible, is carried out by the same body preparing the political aspects of the dialogue.

Political dialogue processes need extensive administrative, logistical, and expert support. This support tends to cover the following areas:

- Logistical issues: transportation and accommodation of participants; servicing of the venue(s); and security.
- Secretarial issues: note taking; information sharing among the dialogue participants; management of documentation; and archiving.
- Expert support: advice on technical and substantive issues through presentations by experts, submissions of papers, or seminars; and, training.
- Media relations and public outreach: providing footage to the media, managing a website, organizing public information campaigns, setting up information points throughout the country, preparing debates on television, etc.

Usually, a secretariat capacity is established prior to the launch of the political dialogue.

Public awareness and participation

When the public is well-informed about the discussions taking place during a political dialogue, the dialogue is likely to be trusted and to enjoy greater legitimacy. Therefore, transparency and information sharing strengthen the legitimacy of a national dialogue process. When designing a public information and awareness-raising strategy, it is important to ensure that the information reaches as wide of a spectrum of society as possible. For example, if a country has high rates of illiteracy, information needs to be shared through media that reach the illiterate population. Similarly, if in certain parts of a country certain information media are not available, the appropriate media need to be identified.

Additionally, the public could be engaged in the discussions of the political dialogue. This may take place through large town hall gatherings or smaller meetings with specific constituencies. It may also include the submission of proposals to the dialogue by civil society and other groups.

Political dialogues benefit from a dedicated body, usually located inside the secretariat supporting the dialogue, which carries out the various public information and participation activities.

Conclusion

Designing peace processes requires difficult decisions on what needs to be discussed and resolved, on who needs to participate, and on what formats the parties feel comfortable with. During peace processes, agendas, formats, and participants frequently change in response to political and military developments. Flexibility and creativity are therefore essential ingredients in the success of a process. It is wise for third parties to avoid using a blueprint when they work with parties to design a peace process, and instead to create bespoke processes for each conflict.

Notes

1 For various definitions of national dialogues, see: "National Dialogue Handbook". See also Murray; Siebert; Harlander; and Papagianni "National Dialogue Processes".
2 Presidential Decree no. 30 (2012) on the Technical Committee for the National Dialogue Conference (author's files).
3 "Final Report of the Technical Committee to Prepare for a Comprehensive National Dialogue Conference" (author's files).

Bibliography

Gervais, Myriam. "Niger: Regime Change, Economic Crisis, and Perpetuation of Privilege". *Political Reform in Francophone Africa*, edited by John F. Clark and David E. Gardinier, Westview Press, 1997, pp. 86–108.

Harlander, Jonathan. "Supporting a National Dialogue; Dilemmas and Options for Third Parties". *Mediation Practice Series*, no. 6, Centre for Humanitarian Dialogue, Dec. 2016.

Heilbrunn, John R. "Social Origins of National Conferences in Benin and Togo". *The Journal of Modern African Studies*, vol. 31, no. 2, June 1993, pp. 277–299.

Murray, Christina. "National Dialogues and Constitution Making". National Dialogue Handbook Background Papers, no. 2, Berghof Foundation, Feb. 2017.

"National Dialogue Handbook; a Guide for Practitioners". Berghof Foundation, 2017, www.berghof-foundation.org.

"Niger Further Details on National Conference". BBC Summary of World Broadcasts, 23 July 1991.

"Niger National Conference Postponed". BBC Summary of World Broadcasts, 27 May 1991.

Nwajiaku, Kathryn. "The National Conferences in Benin and Togo Revisited". *The Journal of Modern African Studies*, vol. 32, no. 3, Sept. 1994, pp. 429–447.

Papagianni, Katia. "National Conferences in Transitional Periods: The Case of Iraq". *International Peacekeeping*, vol. 13, no. 3, 2006, pp. 316–333.

———. "National Dialogue Processes in Political Transitions". Civil Society Dialogue Network Discussion Paper*s*, no. 3, European Peacebuilding Liaison Office (EPLO), Dec. 2013.

Siebert, Hannes. "National Dialogue and Legitimate Change". "Legitimacy and Peace Processes: from Coercion to Consent", Accord, no. 25, Apr. 2014.

Wiseman, John A. *The New Struggle for Democracy in Africa*. Avebury, 1996.

7 China and mediation

Principles and practice

Tiewa Liu[1]

Introduction

Article 33 of the UN Charter states that

> the parties to any dispute, the continuance of which is likely to
> endanger the maintenance of international peace and security, shall,
> first of all, seek a solution by negotiation, enquiry, mediation, con-
> ciliation, arbitration, judicial settlement, resort to regional agencies
> or arrangements, or other peaceful means of their own choice.
>
> (United Nations "UN Charter")

Third-party actions range from fact finding, facilitation, mediation,
arbitration, and adjudication to intervention, including use of force.[2]
Mediation is placed in the middle of the above mentioned approaches,
with an almost perfect combination of intensity and amiability.

However, long before mediation appeared in the UN Charter as an
effective approach to conflict prevention, management, and resolution,
China used the approach of Confucius' "harmony as the instrumen-
tality" to resolve disputes through moral persuasion and consultation
rather than coercion. Chinese approaches to mediation diplomacy
emphasize Confucian morality in relation to social harmony, moder-
ation, respect for authority, humility, and benevolence, in contrast to
the individualistic utilitarian value system of fairness, justice, equality,
equity, and autonomy in Western cultures.[3]

This chapter uses a Confucian lens to elaborate on China's basic
principles of mediation and provide more evidence-based analysis
through a case study of China's mediation in Syria as a means to discuss China's engagement, limitation, and contribution to mediation.
As China is becoming a more important player in international mediation, it is pertinent and necessary to review and generalize the Chinese

approach to mediation, which features in the balance between international responsibility and national interests, and in adherence to the non-interference and non-use of force principle with inclusive and incremental measures.

Categories and effectiveness of mediation

Mediation is categorized into three types. First, *facilitative mediation* sees the mediator structure a process to assist the parties in reaching a mutually agreeable resolution. The mediator does not have any particular interests in either side or leverage to press the outcome of the negotiation; therefore, the mediator will not provide any context to the conflicts but will enable an environment and platform for the parties to negotiate their own solutions to end the conflict. Second, *evaluative mediation* has the mediator make formal or informal recommendations to the parties as to the outcome of the issues (Zumeta). The mediator will practice shuttle diplomacy to separately meet with parties. In addition, the mediator will assist both sides to analyze their costs and benefits of confrontation or a peacefully negotiated agreement. Third, *transformative mediation* sees the mediator possibly utilize "carrots" or "sticks" to ensure recognition of the other side's requests, preventing neglect of the other's interests during the mediation process.

UN practice and effectiveness of mediation

With the complexity and intensity of conflicts dramatically increasing in recent years, the most critical cornerstone for the United Nations was the establishment of the Mediation Support Unit (MSU) within the Policy and Mediation Division (PMD) of the UN Department of Political Affairs (DPA) and, within the unit, the creation of the Standby Team of Senior Mediation Advisers ("Mediation Support Overview").

In relation to the evaluation of effectiveness, MSU published the *UN Guidance for Effective Mediation*, which lists five basic challenges that mediators have to confront as "mission and mandate, impartiality and inclusivity, entry, and consent, strategy, and leverage" (United Nations *United Nations Guidance* 5). These challenges can be translated into three decision-points: the parties are willing to be mediated at the entry level; respect for the mediator and best practices of mediation at the operational level; and consensus at the regional and international levels to facilitate the mediation and increase its rate of success.

Key factors – like preparedness, consent, impartiality, inclusivity, national ownership, coherence, quality peace agreements, international law, and normative frameworks – all support the effective accomplishment of mediation.[4] Therefore, effective mediation embodies full preparation and consent from the parties in conflict; the mediator's impartial engagement under a universally accepted international law framework (fundamentally the UN Charter and other relevant resolutions); and inclusion of the relevant conflict parties and wider society to reach quality peace agreements. While, in practice, the knowledge and the impartiality of the mediator, the labor division, and the ultimate outcome of the mediation might be challenged, these relevant factors still need to be further examined.

Basic principles in China's mediation

Beyond the several rounds of Six-Party Talks regarding the Korean Peninsula, China extends offers to mediate conflict in Saudi Arabia and Iran, India and Pakistan over Kashmir, Afghanistan and Pakistan, Djibouti and Eritrea, Myanmar and Bangladesh, and the Persian Gulf states and Qatar. China is driven by the need to protect its economic investments, a desire to raise its international stature, and a recognition of its responsibilities as a rising power. These all create an increasing impetus for China to adapt its long-held principle of non-interference to demonstrate its capability in international conflict resolution. To be more specific, these realities and intentions indicate that China, in most cases, will still adopt facilitative mediation, as China sticks to the non-interference principle. However, given cautious assessment of the impact of conflicts on China's national interests or international prestige, China will choose to adopt evaluative or transformative mediation when necessary. In terms of the strategic goals and fundamental principles China upholds in mediation, we can concentrate on the aspects described in the following sections.

Balance between national interest and international responsibility

In recent years, under President Xi Jinping's vision and guideline of Chinese diplomacy in the new era, the capability and willingness to build a community of shared future for mankind has required more involvement of China in regional and international negotiations and mediation than before.

In terms of protecting China's national interests, mediation will help safeguard national security. In the case of the Korean Peninsula, China's mediation helped stabilize the situation there, and thus permits China a peaceful environment to sustain its economic development. China's mediation activities have in recent years expanded to the Middle East and African countries. As Xue Li and Zheng Yuwen analyzed it in *The Diplomat*,

> In next decade, the prospect of China's relations with Middle Eastern states mainly lies in the potential for economic cooperation. On the one hand, China wants to play a more significant role in security issues in the Middle East, to show its responsibilities and capabilities as a rising power. On the other hand, China also hopes to get economic and cultural profits from its interactions with the Middle East.
>
> (Xue and Zheng)

Compared with the traditional players like the United States and Russia which prefer to play off one side against the other, or regional powers like Egypt, Turkey, and Saudi Arabia with mixed interests on the ground, or the major international organizations like the United Nations or the Arab League with either limited resources or unrealistic ambitions – China, unlike the other players, "carries no religious, political, historical, and colonial baggage, making it an ideal candidate to break the gridlocks in the region's conflicts and to play the role of an 'honest broker'" (Chaziza). Therefore, China is now striving to balance being an honest broker and mediator in both regional and global conflicts to foster lasting peace and prosperity, and the positive outcome and global stability that China seeks as a rising global power.

Non-interference and non-use of force principle

As early as 2015, Chinese Foreign Minister Wang Yi proposed three principles to address hot issues, namely that

> we adhere to the non-intervention principles into the domestic affairs of the other countries instead of imposing the wills to the others; we insist on the objectivity and impartiality instead of seeking the private interests; we uphold the political solution instead of using the force.
>
> ("Wang Yi")

In academia, there have been several concepts brought forward in this regard, among which Wang Yizhou proposed "creative engagement/intervention", which underlines three aspects: adherence to

UN authority, diplomatic means, and strength in both hard and soft power. Zhao Huasheng advocates for "constructive intervention" to mediate conflicts, as it is reasonable for China to adhere to the non-intervention principle in countries or conflict zones where there is little vital interest or capability to intervene. Others assert that, given that China has critical concerns, interests, and leverages, China should not hesitate to intervene (Zhao). Chiung-Chiu Huang and Chih-yu Shih put forward "harmonious intervention", using "a cultural/civilizational approach to explaining the dynamics of interplay between China's rise and global governance. The key argument [is] that China's quest for security is more centered on the balance of harmonious relations than national interest".[5] Another concept is "deliberative involvement", which means that China, with or without other countries and international organizations, under the principles of state sovereignty and human rights norms, underlines political and diplomatic means to tackle problems. China should consult with parties, and sometimes mediate between opposing parties in conflict, which will help to protect the human rights of the civilians and realize peace (Li Zhiyong "Norm Contestation").

In addition, China insists on the non-interference principle in the cognate fields of peacekeeping and the responsibility to protect. As Mordechai Chaziza observes, "China's mediation diplomacy is part of a carefully devised strategy that suits the country's non-intervention policy framework" (Chaziza). Though China would have the capability to intervene, it still is not willing to intervene with coercive means or a military approach, but rather is aiming at conflict management instead of conflict resolution. In practice, due to the peaceful and non-confrontational positions China takes, China is sometimes the "only mediator that can bring all the opponents to the negotiating table, as it did in the case of Afghanistan" (Putz).

Inclusive and incremental approach to reinforce mediation

The World Bank states that "Each conflict is unique, rooted in local grievances and resentments. Yet the conflicts that have the greatest risk of escalating to violence tend to play out in arenas where access to power, resources, justice, and security are negotiated."[6] That report thus illustrates the necessity to include community structures, traditional leadership, civil society, and private sector to address conflicts more effectively and smoothly. More significantly, the report further proposes three elements to better practice conflict prevention and mediation: national actors; the addressing of grievances through incentives, including investments and medium- or long-term institutional reforms; and the formation of local–global, governmental–non-governmental, public–private coalitions (World Bank and United Nations 23). In practice, China advocates an incremental approach in the mediation process, emphasizing the critical role of the state actor, investment, and longer-term institutional reforms to ensure comprehensive, long-term solutions. A good example is that China encourages regime improvement rather than regime change. For example, during the seven official visits by Kim Jong-il to Beijing, besides the denuclearization and security issues, itineraries included visits to high-tech corporations and economically prosperous zones. To better engage DPRK (the Democratic People's Republic of Korea) in peace talks, China demonstrates the post-Reform and Opening development of China, as an example for the DPRK. However, China's mediation efforts still have some limitations, and most of the engagement still remains in initial phases, and most likely in the track of facilitative mediation through hosting, convening, and facilitating meetings, rather than more assertively exerting its influence through evaluative mediation or transformative mediation.

The case of China's mediation in Syria

Compared with Western countries, China started to engage in international mediation relatively late and with a limited geographical scope. China's role as a mediator in the ongoing Syria crisis, as well as the other conflicts in the Middle East, has extended Chinese willingness, interests, and mediation capacity in the past decades. Therefore, I shall examine the Syria case to detail Chinese policies and practice as a mediator.

Generally speaking, the conflicts in the Middle East can be categorized into four types: conflict between Middle East countries and extra-regional powers; conflict between individual Middle East countries; conflict within individual Middle East countries; and trans-regional conflicts. China is increasingly involved in the first three types of conflict management. The main implementation mechanisms of China include the special envoy of the Ministry of Foreign Affairs; the maritime escort and peacekeeping units of the Ministry of National Defense; and economic assistance through the Ministry of Commerce. Internationally, the China–Arab States Cooperation Forum, Forum of China–Africa Cooperation, the United Nations, and the other international organizations are the international platforms through which China engages in Middle East conflicts (Sun 79).

In regard to the Syria crisis, China appointed a special envoy and took on a supplementary role to the United Nations as the lead mediator.

China emphasized the political and peaceful means and willingness to collaborate with the other regional powers and organizations to cope with the Syria crisis. As China underlines the balance between national powers and responsibilities to the international community, in the Syria case China was inclined to support the image of a responsible great power as trade between China and Syria only amounted to 1.104 billion USD in 2017 ("Zhongguo tong Xuliya"). The special envoy Xie Xiaoyan has been dedicated to the Syria crisis, with multiple visits to Syria to discuss the ongoing situation with parties from both the government and the opposition. In addition, the special envoy has coordinated with countries with greater stakes in Syria, such as Russia, Egypt, Iran, Saudi Arabia, and Lebanon. As the P5 states of the UN Security Council were in disagreement, Special Envoy Xie exchanged ideas with the UN special envoy to Syria frequently in order to address the crisis. After the US strike on Syria this year, Xie participated in the "International Symposium on the Prospect of a Political Settlement of the Syria Issue" co-hosted by SIIS (Shanghai Institute for International Studies) and SISU (Shanghai International Studies University) from May 13 to May 14, 2018, and proposed again that a peaceful and political settlement is the only reliable approach to tackle the issue.

In the initial days of the Syria crisis, China was criticized heavily for its five vetoes, together with Russia. French UN ambassador François Delattre said the failure by the UN Security Council to act would "send a message of impunity" ("Russia and China"). The vetoes were mostly related to the chemical weapons investigation, sanctions, or accusations against the government – a similar pathway that led to the Iraq war with disastrous consequences for both Iraq and the rest of the world. Moreover, China remains cautious about a "coercive" approach from the UN menu, and regime change is a red line which China could not cross in any similar international interventions. Besides, the initial days of the Syria crisis were framed by the consequence of militarized intervention in Libya, which went beyond the writ of UN Security Council Resolution 1973.

More significantly, if we observe the four-point proposal by China and six-point proposal raised by then-UN Special Envoy Kofi Annan, we can better understand China's mediation policy in this issue. Under the UN six-point plan, the Syrian government would commit to work with the UN special envoy (and appoint an interlocutor for the purpose) on a Syrian-led inclusive "political process" addressing the legitimate demands of the Syrian people. The regime was required to immediately cease troop movements and the use of heavy weapons in population centers and begin a pullback of military concentrations in and around them; to permit access to and timely provision of humanitarian assistance to those in need and release prisoners; and to commit to respect freedom of expression and assembly (Hinnebusch and Zartman). On China's side, the four-point plan is as follows:

> Firstly, parties in Syria should make every effort to stop fighting and violence, and cooperate actively with the mediation efforts of Brahimi. Secondly, Syria should appoint empowered interlocutors as soon as possible ... so as to end the Syrian crisis at an early date ... the continuity and effectiveness of Syria's governmental institutions must be maintained. Thirdly, the international community should work with greater urgency and responsibility to fully cooperate with and support Brahimi's mediation efforts ..., Mr. Annan's six-point plan and Security Council resolutions. Fourthly, all parties involved should take concrete steps to ease the humanitarian crisis in Syria.
>
> ("China Announces")

If we compare these two proposals, both plans emphasized no violence; ceasefire; political negotiation; the contribution by the international community, and humanitarian assistance. As the newly released data indicates, China provides emergency humanitarian assistance through both bilateral and multilateral channels to Syrian refugees, totaling 110 million USD. Besides, China also signed an agreement with Syria for an additional 2.5 million US dollars of assistance in the form of buses and customs scanners ("Xu Waizhang"). Moreover, in May 2017, China launched the first Syria post-war reconstruction conference in Beijing, which differed from the approach of other Western countries that attached political reforms to reconstruction assistance. Compared with the regime change proposal by some countries, China underlined "regime improvement" instead and is actively involved in boosting the economic development of the conflict-affected states.

However, Annan's plan mentioned that political prisoners should be released and freedom of expression and assembly should be respected. China particularly underlined that "the continuity and effectiveness of Syria's governmental institutions must be maintained". Therefore, China's plan mostly echoed Annan's proposal while underlining that no regime change should be radically imposed on Syria, so as to realize the transition peacefully and effectively. In addition, China would not pressure the Syrian government in regard to the political prisoners and journalists, which would touch the most sensitive nerve of the Syrian government when there still exist different opposition parties, and confrontation and conflicts among these parties are still going on.

Li Guofu, director of the Center for Middle East Studies at the China Institute of International Studies stated,

> It is time to use China's advantage to promote the talks. We have good relations with the Syrian government. They trust us. On the other side, we have contacts with the opposition, which also believes China holds an objective stance on the Syrian issue.
>
> (Li Xiaokun, "China Takes On")

Other sources echoed this view: "Should China actually host rare peace talks between the Syrian government and opposition, it would be a big step forward in Beijing's direct involvement in ending the messy conflict".[7]

Besides, along with the deterioration of the situation in Syria, the gradual transformation of Chinese policy in this issue should not be overlooked. In October 2016, China for the first time did not align with Russia to veto the Syria draft resolution, which was proposed by France and Spain to halt the bombing of Aleppo, but abstained after presenting a rival draft that urged a ceasefire but made no mention of barring military flights over the city ("Russia's 12 UN Vetoes"). More significantly, though China vetoed a UN resolution, drafted by Britain, France, and the United States, that would have imposed sanctions on Syria over chemical weapons used in the conflict in February 2017, it abstained in a draft resolution demanding President Bashar al-Assad's government cooperate with an investigation into the deadly suspected chemical attack in the rebel-held town of Khan Sheikhun in April, which marked itself as the second greatest turning point for China's position on the Syrian crisis. To some extent, it demonstrates that China, after prudent thinking, would agree to the investigation, with reservations, in order to recover peace and security in Syria. As Courtney Fung elaborates, "China committed to three diplomatic innovations: casting multiple, successive veto vote; rebranding to delegitimize intervention as 'regime change,' and engaging in norm-shaping of the 'responsibility to protect' regarding the use of force" (Fung 693), all of which reflects China's great concerns about regime change and the use of force.

In the most recently delivered speech by special envoy Xie Xiaoyan, China continued to stress the four-point plan, together with a new element, so as to

> continue maintaining communication with all relevant parties; continue supporting the UN's role as the main channel for mediation; continue actively participating in Geneva Peace Talks, the International Syria Support Group and other peace-promotion mechanisms; continue offering assistance within capacity to the Syrian people; support Syria's reconstruction process in proper ways.
>
> ("Special Envoy")

From his speech, we can see that in addition to the four-point plan, China has started to consider the "reconstruction process" in the new phase, which could be counted as a great leap for China from mediation to peacebuilding and sustaining the peace process.

Unfortunately, on April 13, 2018, the United States, the United Kingdom, and France launched airstrikes against Syria, as the United States sought to punish President Assad for a suspected chemical attack near Damascus. Soon after the attack, Chinese UN Ambassador Ma Zhaoxu emphasized Chinese opposition to the unilateral military action and urged "the parties concerned to refrain from any act that could lead to an escalation of the situation, return to the norms of international law and resolve issues through dialogue and consultation". In addition, China again stressed that political settlement is the only way to resolve the situation in Syria. In terms of the Chinese contribution, "China is committed to working with the international community to facilitate peace talks, encourage the cessation of hostilities, violence and counter-terrorism, and advance the process for a political settlement, including through the Intra-Syrian talks" ("Statement by Ambassador Ma Zhaoxu"). Therefore, the non-use of force principle remains the threshold and China is strongly against any military actions without a UN authority and mandate.

Conclusion

With Chinese economic, political, and military development, as well as its national interests spreading more widely in the world, China is currently pursuing a more active role in global governance. In this process, China could further enhance its status as a rising great power and meanwhile consolidate its new type of relationship with the other regional and global powers. As the only developing country in the P5 of the UN Security Council, the attitude and principles China maintains in international intervention will to a great extent shape its future policies in conflict prevention and management. Compared with peacekeeping, which China supports with an increasing scale of personnel and financial contributions, China is cautious about moving forward in other international interventions. Considering mediation demands for resources and leverage, as well as for familiarity with different tools and approaches, China has lacked the motivation and experience to directly participate in mediation before. However, China is incrementally speeding up its involvement in the process, as shown in the Syria crisis. China has, relatively speaking, fewer interests and concerns in Syria, but China has been making great efforts to advocate a leading role for UN mediation as shown through China's veto or abstention behavior. China reserved its veto for its greatest concerns, such as the intervention in domestic political affairs, use of force like airstrikes by the United States and its European allies, and zero-acceptance for regime change.

While China still falls behind in the theory and practice of mediation, it is willing to learn and collaborate with diverse actors, including the conflict parties, regional and global powers, and legitimate regional and international institutions. Maintaining China's fundamental principles of non-intervention and non-use of force, China is currently working on integrating facilitative, evaluative, and transformative measures, to incrementally improve conditions. This approach ensures that mediation is more successful, balancing China's national interests and international responsibilities in the long run.

Notes

1 Tiewa Liu is the Associate Professor of Beijing Foreign Studies University. The author would like to express her great gratitude for a series of workshops kindly sponsored and organized by the Quaker United Nations Office (QUNO), the American Friends Service Committee (AFSC), and the Swiss FDFA, which provided the author support for this research. She also owes thanks for the invitation from Jennifer Staats to a mediation training course sponsored by the United States Institute of Peace (USIP) in 2017 and for Professor Pamela Aall's elaboration and organization of the training which became a valuable asset in this research. Special thanks also go to Dr. Courtney Fung for her professional and insightful advice in the revision of this chapter.

2 From the training course materials delivered by Professor Pamela Aall in USIP.

3   Li Zhaoxing, "Peace, Development and Cooperation-Banner", adapted from Chaziza.
4   For more details about the indicators, please refer to United Nations, *The United Nations Guidance* 4.
5   From a review of the book by Samuel S. Kim. For more information on the book, please refer to Huang and Shih.
6   "Pathways for Peace Inclusive Approaches to Preventing Violent Conflict: Main Messages and Emerging Policy Directions", e-copy from a World Bank publication the author received as reading materials in a workshop organized by the Quaker United Nations Office (QUNO), the American Friends Service Committee (AFSC), and the Swiss FDFA, p. 19.
7   Li Xiaokun, quoting Tokyo-based online magazine, *The Diplomat*.

Bibliography

Chaziza, Mordechai. "China's Approach to Mediation in the Middle East: Between Conflict Resolution and Conflict Management". Middle East Institute, 8 May 2018, www.mei.edu/publications/chinas-approach-mediation-middle-east-between-conflict-resolution-and-conflict.
"China Announces New Proposal on Syria". People.cn, 1 Nov. 2012, http://en.people.cn/90883/8000327.html.
Fung, Courtney J. "Separating Intervention from Regime Change: China's Diplomatic Innovations at the UN Security Council Regarding the Syria Crisis". *The China Quarterly*, vol. 235, 2018, pp. 693–712.
Hinnebusch, Raymond, and I. William Zartman. "UN Mediation in the Syrian Crisis: From Kofi Annan to Lakhdar Brahimi". International Peace Institute, Mar. 2016, www.ipinst.org/wp-content/uploads/2016/03/IPI-Rpt-Syrian-Crisis2.pdf.
Huang, Chiung-Chiu, and Chih-yu Shih. *Harmonious Intervention: China's Quest for Relational Security*. Routledge, 2010.
Li, Xiaokun. "China Takes On Mediation Role". *China Daily*, 24 Dec. 2015, http://europe.chinadaily.com.cn/china/2015-12/24/content_22792541.htm.
Li, Zhaoxing. "Peace, Development and Cooperation-Banner for China's Diplomacy in the New Era". *Chinese Journal of International Law*, vol. 4, no. 2, 2005, pp. 677–683.
Li, Zhiyong. "Norm Contestation and Deliberative Involvement: Chinese Remodeling of the Non-Interference Norm". *Journal of Contemporary Asia-Pacific Studies*, no. 3, 2015, pp. 130–155.
"Mediation Support Overview". *United Nations Peacemaker*, https://peacemaker.un.org/mediation-support.
"Pandian: Chong Wen Jin Zhengri de Lici Fang Hua Zuji" [Summary: Reviewing Kim Jong Il's previous visits to China]. People.cn, 19 Dec. 2011, http://world.people.com.cn/GB/16648603.html.
Putz, Catherine. "Can China Help Mediate between Afghanistan and Pakistan?" *The Diplomat*, 13 June 2017, https://thediplomat.com/2017/06/can-china-help-mediate-between-afghanistan-and-pakistan/.

"Russia and China Veto UN Resolution to Impose Sanctions on Syria". *The Guardian*, 28 Feb. 2017, www.theguardian.com/world/2017/mar/01/russia-and-china-veto-un-resolution-to-impose-sanctions-on-syria.

"Russia's 12 UN Vetoes on Syria". *Raidió Teilifís Éireann*, 11 Apr. 2018, www.rte.ie/news/world/2018/0411/953637-russia-syria-un-veto/.

"Special Envoy of the Chinese Government on the Syrian Issue Xie Xiaoyan Attends International Symposium on the Syrian Issue". Ministry of Foreign Affairs, the People's Republic of China, 14 May 2018, www.fmprc.gov.cn/mfa_eng/wjbxw/t1559820.shtml.

"Statement by Ambassador MA Zhaoxu at the Security Council Briefing on Syria". Permanent Mission of the People's Republic of China to the UN, 17 Apr. 2018, www.china-un.org/eng/hyyfy/t1555285.htm.

Sun, Degang. "Theory and Practice of China's Participation in the Middle East Conflict Governance". *West Asia and Africa*, no. 4, 2015.

United Nations. "UN Charter (full text)". United Nations, www.un.org/en/sections/un-charter/un-charter-full-text/.

———. *The United Nations Guidance for Effective Mediation*. Policy and Mediation Division of the Department of Political Affairs, 2012, https://peacemaker.un.org/sites/peacemaker.un.org/files/GuidanceEffectiveMediation_UNDPA2012%28english%29_0.pdf.

"Wang Yi: Zhongguo Changdao Bing Jian Xing 'Jiejue Redian Wenti San Yuanze'" [Wang Yi: China Advocates and Practises the "Three Principles for Solving Hot Issues"]. People.cn, 23 Mar. 2015, http://world.people.com.cn/n/2015/0323/c157278-26737512.html.

Wang, Yizhou. *Creative Involvement: A New Direction in China's Diplomacy*. Beijing, Beijing UP, 2011.

World Bank and United Nations. *Pathways for Peace: Inclusive Approaches to Preventing Violent Conflict: Main Messages and Emerging Policy Directions*. World Bank, 2017.

"Xu Waizhang: Xuliya Zhanshi Zouxiang Weisheng Zhongguo yuan Canyu Xvliya chongjian" [Syria War is Going to the End and China Would Like to Participate in the Post-War Peacebuilding]. *Guanchazhewang*, 4 Sept. 2018, https://military.china.com/critical3/27/20180904/33788315.html.

Xue, Li, and Zheng Yuwen. "The Future of China's Diplomacy in the Middle East". *The Diplomat*, 26 July 2016, https://thediplomat.com/2016/07/the-future-of-chinas-diplomacy-in-the-middle-east/.

Zhao, Huasheng. "Non-Interference in Internal Affair and Constructive Intervention: Reflection on Chinese Policy after the Unrest in Kyrgyzstan". *Journal of Xinjiang Normal University* (Social Sciences), vol. 32, no. 1, Jan. 2011.

"Zhongguo tong Xuliya de Guanxi" [China's Relations with Syria]. Ministry of Foreign Affairs, PRC, Aug. 2018, www.fmprc.gov.cn/chn//gxh/cgb/zcgmzysx/yz/1206_36/1206x1/t6384.htm.

Zumeta, Zena. "Styles of Mediation: Facilitative, Evaluative, and Transformative Mediation". Mediate.com, www.mediate.com/articles/zumeta.cfm.

Part III
Opportunities for peace

8 How to understand the peacebuilding potential of the Belt and Road Initiative

Dongyan Li

Introduction

In his keynote speech at the Belt and Road International Forum in May 2017, President Xi Jinping proposed to build the Belt and Road Initiative (BRI) into a "road for peace". The World Bank and the United Nations also put forward a joint report on the *Pathways for Peace* in 2018, and emphasized that violence and conflict are big obstacles to reaching the Sustainable Development Goals (SDGs) by 2030. Their report argues that conflict prevention is a decisive factor for development and economic cooperation, and indeed central to reducing poverty and achieving shared prosperity (World Bank and United Nations). This report reflects an increasing trend to strengthen the interaction between the peace and development agendas, and to promote cooperation between both sets of actors.

In this context, this chapter explores the peacebuilding potential of BRI and how to understand the possible connection between BRI and UN peacebuilding. BRI has peacebuilding potential in many aspects, but these potentials are limited at the current stage and uncertain in the future. International efforts are a necessary condition for promoting BRI to contribute more to peacebuilding. The chapter consists of three main sections. First, it explains the core of BRI, which is an economic cooperation–focused initiative, not a peacebuilding initiative; second, it interprets the peace connection and peacebuilding potential of BRI; third, it analyzes the limitations and uncertainties of the peacebuilding potential of BRI, and tries to predict the possible scenarios.

The Belt and Road: an economic cooperation initiative

There are different interpretations and expectations for BRI both internationally and domestically. In China, the mainstream view suggests that BRI should be an economic cooperation initiative, because economic cooperation is easier to carry out. If BRI involves security and peace issues, it will potentially become more complicated or sensitive. BRI is the abbreviation of the "Silk Road Economic Belt" and "21st Century Maritime Silk Road". Considering that the countries along the "Belt and Road" have different resources and strong economic complementarity, there is great potential for economic cooperation. The main contents of BRI are the connectivity in five areas: policy, infrastructure, trade, finance, and people-to-people relations. In the five areas, infrastructure is emphasized first, including investment in factories, roads, bridges, ports, airports, and power grids, as well as communication networks and oil and gas pipeline networks. It is very clear that economic cooperation is the core content of the Belt and Road (*Vision and Actions*).

The mainstream view in China believes that China's advantage lies in economic and development cooperation, so BRI should focus on cooperation in both the economic and development fields:

> The Belt and Road Initiative is an economic behavior, and it is a platform for economic cooperation. It does not involve politics, security, and other fields. Such a choice may help eliminate the external worries about the expansion of China's political and military power and will be beneficial to international co-operation and strategic mutual trust.
>
> (Li Ziguo "Belt and Road Initiative")

According to the official documents, BRI will be promoted by bilateral or multilateral economic cooperation, with special emphasis on the role of both international and domestic markets. In May 2017, the Joint Communique of the Belt and Road Forum for International Cooperation put forward the basic principles of the Belt and Road, and one of the principles is "market-led behavior", that is "recognizing the role of the market and that of business as key players, while ensuring that the government performs its proper role and highlighting the importance of open, transparent, and non-discriminatory procurement procedures" ("Joint Communique").

The Communique emphasized the need to fully understand the role of the market and the status of enterprise as the main body of BRI. This means that the driving force of BRI is not government, but enterprise, and the role of the government is to build the platform for enterprise to flourish. Therefore, the mainstream view sees BRI as separate from peace and security cooperation initiatives, as BRI is a series of market-led economic cooperation projects, themselves distinct from China's foreign aid projects.

The Belt and Road: a road for peace

According to the official definition, BRI is an economic cooperation initiative, aimed at building an economic cooperation platform, and focusing on infrastructure connectivity. But on the other hand, this initiative has an intrinsic and extendable UN peacebuilding link. BRI depends on a peaceful environment. Consolidating peace and sustaining peace are the needs of BRI itself. To this end, BRI economic cooperation can be a driving force for China to promote peace.

Along with the advancement of BRI, the connections between BRI and the United Nations global agendas, including the 2030 Agenda, the refugee, and the migration agendas, as well as the UN peace agenda, are getting closer. Existing research points out the security risks and challenges facing the Belt and Road, noting that along with the continued advancement of BRI, peace and security issues will be more prominent. The three elements of economy, politics, and security are closely interlinked and complementary (Wu 17–22).

There are three major categories of security risks. The first category of risk is the problem of political and social unrest resulting from both domestic and international causes such as slow economic development, serious social injustice, ethnic and religious conflicts, as well as regional power struggles. For example, countries such as Myanmar, Pakistan, and Kyrgyzstan face political instability. The West Asian and North African countries like Libya, Iran, Iraq, Afghanistan, Syria, and Yemen are suffering serious domestic unrest and conflict. The second category of risk is from the "three forces": extremism, terrorism, and separatism. The areas and countries along the Belt and Road are the areas with most active "three forces" caused by ethnic and religious strife. In these areas, terrorism and transnational crime are particularly serious. The third category of risk is geopolitical risk, including the tensions between major powers and the tensions between regional countries. Eurasia is also a conflict-prone area with many disputes in territorial and territorial water disputes (Wu 20–22; Xue "Diplomatic Risks" 68–79).

In China, BRI risk studies increasingly realize that, in addition to conflicts between countries, conflict risks are also emerging from the relations between actors at different levels including governmental actors and non-governmental actors. BRI is a multi-actor project involving the central government, local governments, enterprises and different interest groups both in China and in BRI countries. Due to different interests, there are contradictions and conflicts between different actors, and China is facing increasing tensions in international economic cooperation. For example, Chinese companies in Pakistan and some African countries have been frequently attacked; China's infrastructure projects in Myanmar, Sri Lanka, and Vietnam are protested against by anti-government factions, businessmen, and NGOs in these countries. China's economic cooperation with Myanmar is a typical case that reflects mixed and intertwined conflicts, including the conflict between the central government of Myanmar and local armed forces, the conflict between Chinese businessmen and Myanmar businessmen, as well as the conflict between local NGOs and Chinese companies. This situation suggests that BRI requires risk prevention.

BRI places great emphasis on the importance of establishing and maintaining a peaceful environment. In his keynote speech at the Belt and Road International Forum in May 2017, Xi Jinping proposed building the Belt and Road into "five roads", the first of the "five roads" being "a road for peace". President Xi emphasized that "the ancient silk routes thrived in times of peace, but lost vigor in times of war. The pursuit of the Belt and Road Initiative requires a peaceful and stable environment" ("Full Text of President Xi's Speech"). For the first time, China officially linked the Belt and Road to peace. This means that China needs a peaceful environment in order to achieve the development of BRI and that China is willing to promote world peace through the Belt and Road (Xu 173–174). In 2017, the Joint Communique of the Belt and Road Forum for International Cooperation reiterated the principle of peace and made a commitment to promoting peace and mutually beneficial cooperation.

For building the road for peace, the following principles have been put forward: (1) foster a common, comprehensive, cooperative and sustainable security; (2) create a security environment shared by all; (3) resolve hotspot issues through political means, and promote mediation; (4) enhance counter-terrorism; (5) strive to eradicate poverty and social injustice; and (6) build a new type of international relations based on win–win cooperation (Full Text of President Xi's Speech). Based on these principles, it is possible to put forward some specific actions and measures to build the "road for peace" in the process of BRI.

Obviously, China's statements and commitments cannot eliminate the view of a "China threat". Both within and outside China, there are different interpretations and understandings of the Belt and Road. One of the popular arguments is that the purpose of China's Belt and Road is to expand China's political and military power globally (Bowen). However, despite these critical dismissals, we cannot deny the possibilities that BRI can bring about opportunities for peace, and we cannot deny the possibilities of strengthening the links between BRI and peacebuilding. China expresses the political will for peace promotion, and there is also a strong motivation for China to promote and sustain peace in the Belt and Road countries. Therefore, a positive approach is to promote the Belt and Road to contribute to conflict prevention and peacebuilding.

The peacebuilding potential of the Belt and Road

With regard to concepts, UN peacebuilding is a part of UN peace operations. According to the UN resolutions on the establishment of the Peacebuilding Commission, peacebuilding activities are aimed at assisting countries emerging from conflict, reducing the risk of relapsing into conflict, and laying the foundation for sustainable peace and development (*Peacebuilding Commission*).There are four core elements of peacebuilding.

1. Peacebuilding activities are aimed at post-conflict countries rather than the building of broad-based international peace.
2. The purposes of peacebuilding are preventing post-conflict countries from falling into conflict again and laying a foundation for sustainable peace and development.
3. Peacebuilding emphasizes the interaction of institutional reform, development, human rights, and peace, with broad missions including reintegrating former combatants into civilian society, strengthening the rule of law, improving human rights, assisting elections, promoting conflict resolution, and reconciliation techniques (*Report of the Panel*).
4. Peacebuilding emphasizes the multi-actor partnerships among governments, international organizations, non-governmental organizations, and the private sector, with special emphasis on the role of civil society organizations and women's participation (*Peacebuilding Commission*).

The nature of BRI is different from UN peacebuilding and the "Pathway for Peace" proposed by the United Nations and the World Bank. BRI is solely an initiative of China, not part of the agenda of international organizations. BRI adopts a cooperative approach based on voluntary and equal consultation, not a third-party intervention approach, and non-interference remains a major principle of China. As an economic cooperation initiative, BRI does not include the peacebuilding missions like institution building and elections assistance. However, from a Chinese perspective, there are three overlaps between BRI and UN peacebuilding.

First, many of the countries covered by peacebuilding projects, such as Kyrgyzstan, Lebanon, Myanmar, Philippines, Sri Lanka, Tajikistan, and Yemen, are also participating countries of BRI. Second, UN peacebuilding activities are very broad and there is room for cooperation with Belt and Road. One of Secretary-General Boutros Boutros-Ghali's peacebuilding projects is to bring states together in joint programmes to develop agriculture, improve transportation, or utilize resources such as water or electricity that they need to share. He believed that this would be a way to reduce hostile perception and promote reconciliation (*Agenda for Peace*). In defining the concept of peacebuilding, the Brahimi Report believes that peacebuilding also includes the implementation of humanitarian demining programmes, emphasis on HIV/AIDS education and control, and action against other infectious diseases. In these respects, BRI has the possibility of cooperation with UN peacebuilding (*Report of the Panel*). Third, some BRI countries face serious conflict risks, and China's efforts to promote peace in these countries will contribute to UN peacebuilding.

The peacebuilding potential of the Belt and Road is prominent in the following aspects.

An inclusive platform that can be used to promote peacebuilding

BRI aims to provide a broad platform for economic cooperation with many layers and possibilities for participation. President Xi Jinping emphasized that China would build more cooperation platforms, and allow all sectors of societies and groups to participate in BRI cooperation, including international organizations, regional organizations, non-governmental organizations, civil society organizations, and think tanks. Since BRI was proposed, China has established Belt and Road cooperation with many international organizations, including UNDP, UNICEF, the Human Settlements Programme, the World Health Organization, the International Committee of the Red Cross, and the International Criminal Police Organization ("Outcome List"). These organizations are also partner organizations related to UN peacebuilding.

Strengthening the exchanges between the people along the Belt and Road is one of the important contents of the Belt and Road Initiative. On the initiative of the Chinese Association of Civil Organizations for Promotion of International Exchanges, a cooperation network of civil society organizations along the Silk Road was established, with more than 160 Chinese and foreign civil organizations now part of this cooperation network. In 2017, this Association, with more than 90 Chinese social organizations, formally launched the Chinese Social Organizations' Action Plan to Promote the Belt and Road Initiative (2017–2020).

Such an inclusive platform for the Belt and Road cooperation can be used as a platform for peacebuilding, especially as a "people for peace" platform. This kind of cooperation network is also a model encouraged by the UN peacebuilding. If the Belt and Road is progressing smoothly, it is very likely to establish partnerships with more peacebuilding-related organizations and agencies, promoting future cooperation between peacebuilding actors and the Belt and Road actors.

Economic and development cooperation for peace

Promoting peace and security through economic and development cooperation is China's consistent notion based on the "China experience". China attaches importance to development and peace and actively supports the 2030 Agenda, and emphasizes the high degree of connectivity between BRI and the 2030 Agenda. The Joint Communique of the Belt and Road International Forum mentioned that the 2030 Agenda with the set of Sustainable Development Goals provided a new blueprint of international cooperation. While emphasizing the decisive role of conflict prevention for economic development, UN peacebuilding reports also emphasized the interlinked relations between peace, development, and human rights. Development is obviously a relevant element of peacebuilding. One realistic approach for China's "development for peace" is to establish a closer interconnection between BRI and the sixteenth goal of the 2030 Agenda – to promote peaceful and inclusive societies – as well as the interconnection between the Belt and Road and UN peacebuilding. Strengthening the cooperation between development actors and peacebuilding actors is a possible direction of China "development for peace" and the BRI "road for peace". For example, youth and women's employment is included in UN peacebuilding, and China can provide support for youth and women's employment in Belt and Road countries through BRI projects.

The International Committee of the Red Cross is one of the Belt and Road partners, and emphasizes the mutual benefits of social stability and development. Specific infrastructure construction and personnel training projects led by the ICRC have the potential to supplement the Belt and Road. For example, ICRC fixes and sets up water and energy infrastructure, supports hospitals and orthopedic centers, trains locals to develop skills, and helps people start sustainable small businesses (Maurer). China supports the ICRC humanitarian cause, and encourages the Red Cross Society of China to enhance practical cooperation with the ICRC under the BRI framework ("Chinese Vice President").The partnership between the ICRC and BRI can be the model for other peacebuilding actors.

Enhance capacity of peacebuilding

The cooperation between China and the countries along the Belt and Road has included items related to the enhancement of peacebuilding capacity: (1) economic and development capacity training; (2) peace education and peace training; (3) humanitarian assistance and medical and health training; (4) capacity building for protecting the basic rights of children and women. These are included in the goals of the *Chinese Social Organizations' Action Plan for Closer People-to-People Bonds along the Belt and Road (2017–2020)* and can be expanded to more aspects related to peacebuilding (Chinese Social Organizations' Action Plan). The Action Plan made a commitment to "maintaining peace and security in the regions along the Belt and Road". The Action Plan also mentioned that Chinese social organizations would organize activities like international peace day, peace forum, and peace education, and make contact with the local peace organizations along the Belt and Road to jointly maintain the peaceful environment.

In July 2016, the Ministry of Education of China Issued the Belt and Road Education Action Plan, which involves different governmental and non-governmental actors as well as different aspects of education and training projects. For example, the Belt and Road Education Action Plan mentioned that "we will also boost implementation of youth exchange programs along the Silk Road", and "we will deepen cooperation on cultivation and training of talent. Such multi-layered cooperation in vocational and technical education will help to cultivate the different kinds of talent that are much needed by the Belt and Road countries" (*Education Action Plan*). The Belt and Road Education Action Plan emphasized that "it is our shared responsibility to strengthen the pillars of regional peace through educational cooperation and exchange and thereby expanding people-to-people exchanges" (*Education Action Plan*).

Conflict prevention or peacebuilding is a broad concept, including issues like restoring economy, youth employment, and combating transnational crimes and counter-terrorism. BRI can provide some support in these areas. One possibility is that BRI can provide "hard support" to "soft peacebuilding", for example, the infrastructure support for peacebuilding-related training, education, and research.

Limitation and uncertainty

As mentioned above, in many aspects, BRI has potential for promoting peacebuilding, and it is possible to establish a complementary relationship between the Belt and Road actors and peacebuilding actors. However, the link between BRI and peacebuilding is still limited and uncertain, and BRI has not established official connection with UN peacebuilding.

Development for peace, not peace for development

Despite the recognition of the interactions between development and peace, the major peacebuilding potential of BRI is promoting peace through economic and development cooperation, rather than promoting development through peace operation or conflict prevention. Both UN peacebuilding and BRI have emphasized the interconnection between development and peace, but they each have a different focus and priority. UN peacebuilding is a broader concept, and pays great attention to political affairs, especially supporting national efforts to establish, redevelop, or reform institutions. Unlike the UN peacebuilding agenda, BRI puts economic and development cooperation first, and takes infrastructure as a priority. So BRI will choose peaceful and stable countries to promote economic cooperation. As an economic cooperation initiative, the peacebuilding contribution of BRI is limited.

Unfavorable factors, uncertain outcomes

The progress of BRI is affected by both internal factors and international factors. Relations between big powers, cross–Taiwan strait relations, the South China Sea issue, and China's relations with neighboring countries are regarded as China's core security interests. These are major international and internal factors that may greatly influence BRI (Xue "Diplomatic Risks" 68–79). At present, relations between major powers remain tense. The tension between China and the US military alliance in the Asia-Pacific region is considered to be the most important factor in China's foreign policy. Instabilities in this region will contain China's investment in the Belt and Road Initiative and peacebuilding. China's political will and capability to increase the investment in the Belt and Road and UN peacebuilding depend on these factors.

BRI will give priority to countries with good political relations and willingness to cooperate with China, as well as countries with a stable environment. A good international political relationship will lead to smooth progress of economic cooperation. In turn, smooth economic cooperation will contribute to peace and security cooperation, including further cooperation in non-traditional security issues, like the cooperation in the fields of combating and preventing transnational crime, human trafficking, corruption, as well as anti-terrorism. This is an ideal scenario of BRI cooperation. However, not all countries along the Belt and Road have such an ideal political environment and condition, and there are many unfavorable factors that will affect the progress of the Belt and Road. Officially, BRI is still an economic cooperation initiative without established goals and schedules. In the Chinese language, "initiative" is a word with more flexibility and ambiguity compared to words such as "strategy" or "agenda". If the situation is unfavorable for economic cooperation, BRI will proceed with caution, shrinking in scope and adapting as necessary.

From infrastructure to peacebuilding: necessary conditions are required

The physical infrastructure projects of BRI, like railway construction, road construction, or oil pipeline construction, will not automatically make contributions to peacebuilding. On the one hand, the infrastructure projects can be used for peace purposes – such as election venues, media centers, or hospitals, which China has already done through its infrastructure projects under the flag of UN peacekeeping. On the other hand, infrastructure projects may even be the cause of domestic or international disputes, as mentioned above. In addition, Belt and Road projects themselves also face various security risks, including the threat from terrorism.

The current situation is that the enterprises lack peacebuilding awareness and knowledge, and infrastructure projects cannot automatically contribute to peacebuilding. Some necessary conditions are required for promoting BRI infrastructure projects to contribute to peacebuilding. The necessary conditions include: establishing a connection between the Belt and Road Initiative and UN peacebuilding, adding concrete peacebuilding arrangements to BRI, promoting cooperation between BRI and peacebuilding, and enhancing the active interaction between the Belt and Road actors and peacebuilding actors.

China's willingness is obviously a decisive factor, but the position of relevant countries and international organizations is also indispensable. With regard to peacebuilding, the influence of international factors is more prominent, the enhancement of the interconnection between the Belt and Road and peacebuilding depending mainly on the promotion of external factors, including the efforts of the United Nations and regional organization. If the Belt and Road goes smoothly, and the peacebuilding efforts of international organizations are strong enough, it is very likely that the Belt and Road will make a greater contribution to peacebuilding. If China's political will and enthusiasm decline, or the Belt and Road process slows down or shrinks, the peacebuilding potential of BRI will also decline.

The United Nations has its own intellectual advantages and practical experience in the areas of peacebuilding, supplementing gaps in the BRI. However, it remains necessary for UN agencies to take more active steps to cooperate with BRI in peacebuilding, and help to establish the interconnection between economic cooperation and peacebuilding. Joint projects between the United Nations, Chinese Belt and Road actors, and the Belt and Road countries should be promoted. These efforts could include training, research, and economic cooperation programs. UN agencies should do more to enhance cooperative relations between the UN Pathways for Peace and the Belt and Road for Peace.

Conclusion

Peacebuilding is a comprehensive concept including development-related issues. UN peacebuilding emphasizes the interlinkages between peace, development, and human rights, and calls for strengthening the cooperation between peace actors and development actors. According to the definition of the United Nations, conflict prevention is also a comprehensive prevention that requires an interaction of different measures and actors. From the perspective of UN peacebuilding, BRI, as an economic cooperation–led initiative, could and should make its contribution to UN peacebuilding and conflict prevention. However, at this stage, the BRI peacebuilding potential is still very limited. The BRI peacebuilding potential is constrained and affected by different factors, both "China factors" and "non-China factors", which interact and influence each other. Though BRI has potential for peacebuilding in many aspects, this potential remains conditional and uncertain. BRI is only likely to achieve a positive outcome of peacebuilding through active international cooperation.

Bibliography

An Agenda for Peace. A/47/277- S/24111, United Nations, General Assembly/ Security Council, 17 June 1992, http://www.un.org/zh documents/view_doc. asp?/ symbol=A%2F477&Submit = %E6%90%9 C%E7%B4%A2&Lang=C. Accessed 18 Nov. 2018.

Bai, Yunzhen. "The Belt and Road Initiative and the Transformation of China's Foreign Aid". *World Economics and Politics*, no. 11, 2015, pp. 53–71.

Bowen, James. "China, Global Peacemaker?" *The Global Observatory*, International Peace Institute, 2017, www.ipinst.org/?s=China%2C+Global+Peacemaker. Accessed 28 Aug. 2018.

Call, Charles T., and Cedric de Coning, editors. *Rising Powers and Peacebuilding: Breaking the Mold?* Palgrave MacMillan, 2017.

Chinese Social Organizations' Action Plan for Closer People-to-People Bonds along the Belt and Road (2017–2020). China NGO Network for International Exchanges (CNIE), 14 May 2017, www.cnie.org.cn/WebSite/zlbmj/UpFile/2017/201751716122275.doc. Accessed 1 July 2018.

"Chinese Vice President Pledges to Support ICRC Humanitarian Cause". *xinhuanet.com*, 30 May 2018, www.xinhuanet.com/english/2018-05/30/c_137218100.htm?platform=hootsuite. Accessed 29 Aug. 2018.

Education Action Plan for the Belt and Road Initiative. Ministry of Education of the People's Republic of China, July 2016, https://eng.yidaiyilu.gov.cn/home/rolling/30278.htm. Accessed July 15, 2018.

Flint, Colin, and Zhang Xiaotong. "The Belt and Road and the Innovation of Geopolitical Theory". *Foreign Affairs Review*, no. 3, 2016, pp. 1–24.

"Full Text of President Xi's Speech at Opening of B&R Forum". The State Council Information Office of China, 15 May 2017, www.scio.gov.cn/32618/1552699/1552699.htm /2017-05-15. Accessed 29 Aug. 2018.

Jiang, Heng. "Recognition of Investment Risk in High Conflict Areas: A Case Study of China's Investment in Myanmar". *International Economic Cooperation*, no. 11, 2011, pp. 9–12.

Jin, Ling. "The Belt and Road Initiative: China's Marshall Plan?" *International Studies*, no. 1, 2015, pp. 88–99.

"Joint Communique of the Leaders Roundtable of the Belt and Road Forum for International Cooperation". Ministry of Foreign Affairs, the People's Republic of China, 16 May 2017, www.fmprc.gov.cn/mfa_eng/zxxx_662805/t1462012.shtml. Accessed 28 Aug 2018.

Li, Xiao, and Li Junjiu. "The Belt and Road Initiative and the Reconstruction of China's Geopolitical Economic Strategy". *World Economics and Politics*, no. 10, 2015, pp. 30–59.

Li, Xiao, and Xu Li. "The 21st Century Maritime Silk Road: Security Risks and Counter Measures". *Pacific Journal*, no. 7, 2015, pp. 50–64.

Li, Ziguo. "The Belt and Road Initiative: Achievements, Problems and Ideas". *Eurasian Economy*, no. 4, 2017, pp. 2–18.

———. "The Connectivity Point of the Belt and Road Initiative Vision of People to People". *Journal of Xinjiang Normal University (Edition of Philosophy and Social Sciences)*, no. 3, 2016, pp. 67–74.

Liu, Jangyong. "The Theory of Peace and Harmony between Sea and Land: Geopolitics on the Sustainable Development of the Belt and Road Initiative". *Journal of International Security Studies*, no. 5, 2015, pp. 3–21.

Ma, Yun. "Risk Management and Control in the Construction of the Belt and Road Initiative". *China Review of Political Economy*, no. 4, 2015, pp. 189–203.

Maurer, Peter. "Why There Should Be a Humanitarian Dimension to China's Belt and Road Project". Resource Centre, International Committee of the Red Cross, 2017, www.icrc.org/en/resource-centre/result?t=Why+Th ere+Should+be+a+Humanitarian+Dimension+to+China%27s+Belt+ and+Road+Projec. Accessed 27 Aug. 2018.

Melber, Henning. "'In a Time of Peace Which Is No Peace': Security and Development Fifty Years after Dag Hammarskjöld". *Global Governance*, vol. 18, no. 3, 2012, pp. 267–272.

"Outcome List of the Belt and Road International Cooperation Summit Forum (full text)". Ministry of Foreign Affairs, the People's Republic of China, 16 May 2017, www.fmprc.gov.cn/web/ziliao_674904/1179_674909/t1461873. shtml. Accessed 30 Aug. 2018.

Peacebuilding and Sustaining Peace Report of the Secretary-General. A/72/707-S/2018/43, United Nations, General Assembly/Security Council, 18 January 2018, www.un.org/zh/documents/view_doc.asp?symbol=A/72/707. Accessed 28 July 2018.

The Peacebuilding Commission. A/RES/60/180, United Nations, General Assembly, 30 Dec. 2005, www.un.org/zh/documents/view_doc.asp?symbol =A+%2FRES%2F60%2F180&Submit=%E6%90%9C%E7%B4%A2&Lan g=C. Accessed 18 Nov. 2018.

Report of the Panel on United Nations Peace Operations (Brahimi Report). A/ 55/305-S /2000/809, United Nations, General Assembly/Security Council, 21 Aug. 2000, www.un.org/zh/documents/view_doc.asp?symbol=A%2F5 5%2F305+&Submit=%E6%90%9C%E7%B4%A2&Lang=C. Accessed 18 Nov. 2018.

Tang, Pengqi. "Political and Economic Risks of Implementing the 'One Belt, One Road' Strategy: A Case Study of China's Investment in Sri Lanka". *South Asian Studies Quarterly*, no. 2, 2015, pp. 102–106.

Tardy, Thierry. "Hybrid Peace Operations: Rationale and Challenges". *Global Governance*, vol. 20, no. 1, 2014, pp. 95–118.

Vision and Actions on Jointly Building Silk Road Economic Belt and 21st-Century Maritime Silk Road. National Development and Reform Commission, Ministry of Foreign Affairs, and Ministry of Commerce of the People's Republic of China, People's Publishing House, 2015.

Wang, Yizhou. *Creative Involvement: the Evolution of China's Global Role.* Peking UP, 2013.

World Bank and United Nations. *Pathways for Peace: Inclusive Approaches to Preventing Violent Conflict*. World Bank, 2018, doi:10.1596/ 978-1-4648-1162-3.

Wu, Jiansheng. "Views on Several Problems on the Belt and Road Initiative". *China Development Watch*, no. 6, 2015, pp. 17–22.

Xu, Yanzhuo. "Belt and Road Initiatives in 2017: Development and Achievements". *Annual Report on International Politics and Security (2018)*, edited by Zhang, Yuyan et al. Social Sciences Academic Press (China), 2018, pp. 168–181.

Xue, Li. *The Belt and Road Initiative: Analysis from Chinese and Foreign Scholars*. China Social Sciences Press, 2017

———. "The Diplomatic Risks of China's Belt and Road Strategy". *International Economic Review*, no. 2, 2015, pp. 68–79.

Zhang, Yunling, and Yuan Zhengqing. *The Belt and Road and China's Development Strategy*. Social Sciences Academic Press (China), 2017.

Zhou, Ping. "Management and Control of the Geopolitical Risks of the Belt and Road Initiative". *Exploration and Free Views*, no. 1, 2016, pp. 83–86.

9   Security sector reform and conflict prevention

Albrecht Schnabel

Introduction

Conflict prevention is crucially important for creating stable and safe environments for people and states, for development and business. In two aspects, security sector reform (SSR) is particularly important for conflict prevention. First, SSR helps security institutions, as well as those institutions mandating and overseeing their work, to be in the best possible position to provide effective, efficient, and accountable security in order to prevent the escalation of insecurity and violence. Second, in cases where security institutions are among the very sources of insecurity, they need to be reformed so that they prevent – and not cause – insecurity.

SSR supports conflict prevention, and conflict prevention is an important pillar for peace, stability, and development. Putting it differently, investing in SSR such as developing SSR strategies, programs, and activities and promoting good security sector governance (SSG) principles, supports stability, prevents violent conflicts – both sudden and protracted ones – and sustains safe environments for economic investment, cooperation, and development. Failing to invest in it would be a strategic mistake from both political and economic standpoints. The following pages offer an overview of SSG and SSR, conflict prevention, and the link between them, before reflecting on the Swiss tradition of promoting good SSG globally and on the opportunity for China's Belt and Road Initiative (BRI) to promote good SSG among the countries participating in the BRI.

The security sector, good security sector governance, and security sector reform

The 2008 report on security sector reform by the UN Secretary-General offers a solid framework for a common, comprehensive, and coherent approach by the United Nations and its member states, reflecting shared principles, objectives and guidelines for the development and implementation of SSR (Hänggi and Scherrer 3–4). The report notes that:

> It is generally accepted that the security sector includes defense, law enforcement, corrections, intelligence services and institutions responsible for border management, customs and civil emergencies. Elements of the judicial sector responsible for the adjudication of cases of alleged criminal conduct and misuse of force are, in many instances, also included. Furthermore, the security sector includes actors that play a role in managing and overseeing the design and implementation of security, such as ministries, legislative bodies and civil society groups. Other non-state actors that could be considered part of the security sector include customary or informal authorities and private security services.
>
> (United Nations "Securing Peace and Development" para. 14; OECD/DAC; United Nations Development Programme 87)

As the security sector's main purpose is to provide security as a public service to a state and its population, SSR needs to follow basic good governance principles. What do those principles of "good governance" mean when applied to security institutions? A brief look at some core good governance principles highlights their importance for the security sector:

- *Participation:* Security institutions and their personnel are representative of the population they serve, including women and men, and all ethnic groups.
- *Equity/inclusivity:* All members of society can join the security institutions, are treated equally by them and can participate in commenting on them – they see them as "their institutions" that are providing an important public service.
- *Rule of law:* The impartial enforcement of and adherence to law is crucial; security providers are not above the law and do not enjoy impunity; legal frameworks also must reflect the aspirations and roles of modern and professional security institutions.

- *Transparency:* Civil authorities and civil society actors have access to information about the work of their security institutions.
- *Responsiveness:* The professional and timely delivery of security and justice as a public service can be expected; the institution displays a distinct service-orientation.
- *Consensus orientation:* Coherent policies and responsibilities of the sector are based on inclusive and broad stakeholder consultation processes; ownership, direction, and scope of reforms are broad-based and broadly supported.
- *Effectiveness and efficiency:* Effective and professional management of security institutions and delivery of services is in place, based on a smart use of human capital and financial resources, while available resources match mandates, tasks, and efforts towards meeting good governance principles.
- *Accountability:* Security sector actors provide explanations and justifications, and accept responsibility for actions and decisions; they have structures in place that guarantee internal accountability and accountability to democratic and civilian authorities, as well as civil society organizations.

By promoting good governance principles in reform efforts, security institutions are more accountable to the state and its people; effective, efficient, and affordable; respectful of international norms, standards, and human rights; and considered as legitimate security providers by all stakeholders. They are respected, instead of feared by the people they serve.

The academic and practitioner literature as well as official and operational and institutional statements highlight that meaningful SSR should additionally embrace the following principles:

- SSR should be people-centered, locally owned, and based on democratic norms, human rights principles, and the rule of law, so that it can provide freedom from fear and measurable reductions in armed violence and crime. This principle must be upheld in both the design and the implementation of SSR programs. It should not simply remain at the level of proclamation and intention (Nathan; Donais).
- SSR must be seen as a framework to structure our thinking about how to address diverse security challenges facing states and their populations, through more integrated development and security policies and greater civilian involvement and oversight. National, broad and public consultation processes as well as a national

security strategy are thus inherent requirements of feasible SSR strategies.

- SSR activities should form part of multisectoral strategies, based on broad assessments of the range of security and justice needs of the people and the state. They have to respond to the needs of all stakeholders.

- SSR must be implemented through clear processes and policies that enhance institutional and human capacities to ensure that security policy can function effectively and justice can be delivered equitably (United Nations "Maintenance of International Peace"; European Commission; Council of the European Union; Hänggi).

While various types of reforms could take place (and have always taken place) within the security sector that do not aim at meeting SSG principles, these do not qualify as SSR. Such reforms include traditional train-and-equip activities that are part of military or police reforms outside the remit of SSR. While strengthening the effectiveness of security institutions' performance, such reforms change very little in the way security institutions are run, governed, and perceived not only by the government, but also by the population they serve. Yet, these limited, technical reforms within individual security institutions (such as the military or police) are often preferred over more far-reaching SSR. Experience with close engagement throughout many regions of the world, including Asia, shows that, while the main tenets of SSG and SSR are usually not put in question, SSR sits less comfortably with governments favoring more centralized rule and limited oversight of security institutions by civilian actors. In such contexts, both political and military elites might fully appreciate the principles of SSG and SSR, yet for various reasons they do not want to be subjected to parliamentary oversight or managed by civilian ministries. In such situations, SSR can still focus on sensitization and investment in certain good governance principles, while waiting for a more conducive political environment supporting more far-reaching reforms.

Quite often – and this is the case not only in particularly difficult and challenging SSR environments – skepticism about SSR grows from a feeling that the approach to SSG and SSR needs to be adjusted to a country's cultural, political, and historical contexts. Sometimes the main tenets of SSG and SSR are considered to be unduly influenced by Western or Northern notions of governance and the roles of security institutions in society (Schnabel "Ideal Requirements"). However, extensive engagement in SSG and SSR debates and applications in various regions around the world shows that their main tenets are not rejected as Western/Northern notions. The challenges and responses that necessitate SSR remain very similar, regardless of whether seen from the North or the South: however, while the focus of SSR should be on SSG principles, the scope and sequencing of reforms must be attuned to local contexts and conditions (Aguja and Schnabel). Thus, while the concepts of SSG and SSR are not challenged in their basic foundations, different levels of willingness and preparedness to engage in SSR exist, depending on the nature of the political system, political stability, and economic well-being of the society concerned. As will be argued in more detail below, an effective, efficient and accountable security sector that is able to protect society against internal and external threats makes a strong contribution to internal and external peace and stability.

The need for SSR

Under which circumstances can we assume that a security sector is in need of reform? If the sector is not inclusive, is partial and corrupt, unresponsive, incoherent, ineffective, and inefficient and/or unaccountable to the public, then the sector (or any of its affected institutions) is in need of reform. The term "reform" describes an institutional and procedural transformation of the security sector that leads to improvements in the performance of a legitimate, credible, well-functioning, and well-governed security sector that, as a public service provider, delivers internal and external, direct and structural security.

The extent of the reform required in each specific instance depends on the changes and adaptations required for making the sector fulfill its roles in an efficient and accountable manner, and rarely involves a total overhaul. Some components and aspects of a nation's security sector might be functioning very well, while others might be in need of extensive improvements. Thus, identifying where, how, and when individual institutions might need to be (re)built, restructured, changed, and/or fine-tuned is an important step. It requires a solid assessment of the sector's roles, tasks, and requirements in light of national and local assessments of society's security and development needs. Security sector assessments and SSR planning therefore ideally build on current and realistic national security policies and strategies.

What SSR does

Activities to reform, improve, and adjust a security sector focus on developing an effective, affordable, and efficient security sector, for example by restructuring or improving human and material capacities.

Reforms also include ensuring democratic and civilian control of the security sector, for example through strengthening the management and oversight capacities of government ministries, parliament, and civil society organizations. Thus, referring again to the UN report mentioned earlier in the text, security sector reform

> describes a process of assessment, review and implementation as well as monitoring and evaluation led by national authorities that has as its goal the enhancement of effective and accountable security for the State and its peoples without discrimination and with full respect for human rights and the rule of law.
> (United Nations "Maintenance of International Peace" para. 17)

In operational terms, SSR covers a wide range of activities (Hänggi and Scherrer 15):

* *Overarching activities*, such as security sector reviews and their development, needs assessments, and development of SSR strategies and national security policies.
* *Activities related to security- and justice-providing institutions*, such as restructuring and reforming national defense, police, and other law enforcement agencies as well as judicial and prison systems based on SSR strategies and national security policies.
* *Activities related to civilian management and democratic oversight of security and justice institutions*, including executive management and control, parliamentary oversight, judicial review, oversight by independent oversight bodies and civil society organizations.
* *Activities related to SSR in post-conflict environments*, such as disarmament, demobilization, and reintegration (DDR), control of small arms and light weapons, mine action, and transitional justice.
* *Activities related to cross-cutting concerns*, such as gender issues and child protection.

These SSR activities – and SSR's contribution to peacebuilding and the prevention of violence and armed conflict – have political, economic, social, and institutional dimensions. The political dimension focuses on the promotion and facilitation of civilian and democratic control over security institutions; the economic dimension ensures appropriate allocation and consumption of society's resources for the security sector; the social dimension holds that the provision of the population's physical security should be guaranteed, and not threatened by the security institutions; and, directly related, the institutional dimension focuses on the professionalization of all actors in the security sector (Wulf 5; Schnabel "Security-Development Discourse").

Making the case for pursuing genuine SSR – and regional experiences

The consequences of ineffective and unaccountable security institutions can be detrimental to a society's safety, stability, and security: suspicions and rumors spread about non-transparent security institutions among the public, media, and political decision-makers; human rights abuses and the absence of a proper response to them, and corruption and other misconduct by security institutions, create fear and distrust among the population. Furthermore, poor reputation of security institutions raises doubts about the legitimacy of state institutions in general and reduces society's trust in, and loyalty to, the state and its institutions. Consequently, state and society are more likely to experience political crises, violent conflict, and low human and economic development. Investing in SSR helps tackle those problems and can contribute to reversing such negative tendencies and to mitigating some drivers in the escalation of tensions to open violence. Centralized political systems are less likely to embrace the holistic character of the security sector. By focusing reforms exclusively on security institutions' capacity to strengthen their effectiveness through train-and-equip programs, while leaving aside investments in civilian management and oversight, they do not engage in SSR *per se*. More effective and less accountable security institutions may sway even further from their public duty of security provision and be feared and distrusted by the society they serve.

On the other hand, genuine SSR, embracing efforts to focus on both security provision and civilian oversight, create more effective and accountable security institutions, benefiting society in a number of ways: With more transparent, cost-effective, and legitimate security provision, security institutions are seen as important assets by the population; they enjoy a positive reputation within society and are seen as attractive employers; they bring broad benefits to society in the form of better security provision and the creation of a friendly environment for human and economic development; and they guarantee better protection of rights, security, stability, and rule of law. All of these benefits of SSR are critically important for conflict prevention and post-conflict recovery. Throughout the Asian region, experience shows that honest efforts by governments and security institutions towards strengthening not only their effectiveness through investments in new infrastructure, equipment, and training activities, but also their accountability by investing in better relations with the media, civil society, and parliament have paid off in the short term, as reforms increased their reputation domestically as well as internationally. For instance, international investments have increased. At the same time, in places where reforms slowed down or were reversed, or security institutions were found to have committed major human rights breaches, international investments quickly pulled out.

Throughout the region, movement towards good SSG and subsequent SSR is challenged by a number of factors. In South Asia these include a shortage of independent and strong oversight/management bodies in the security sector; growing terrorist threats and organized crime; long histories of internal conflict; mixed success with DDR of armed non-state groups; or emerging existential and environmental threats. In Southeast Asia, the challenging environment for good SSG and subsequent SSR is characterized by, among other things, praetorian states – security institutions directly and indirectly intervening in politics and civilian leadership, including the military's role in parliament; an absence of independent and strong oversight/management bodies in the security sector; long histories of protracted internal conflicts and dragging peace processes; uneven success with DDR of armed non-state groups; growing terrorist threats, violent religious extremism, and organized crime; attempts by security institutions to crack down on public dissent, despite high "collateral damage" among the civilian population; and a lack of professionalism and SSG expertise in the security sector – among both security institutions and oversight institutions. In East Asia, the challenging environment for good SSG and subsequent SSR is characterized by, among other things, security providers who are accountable to non-pluralist democratic systems and alternative governance structures, as well as politicized security providers and strong presence of military influences in politics; oversight and management bodies in the security sector that are not freely elected; or ongoing armed conflict and the potential for nuclear proliferation.

However, there are also numerous positive developments that contribute to creating an increasingly conducive environment for sustainable SSG/R: There are established democracies in the region with professional security institutions, strong civilian control of security agencies, and solid respect for good governance principles. There is overall a considerable need and demand for SSG and SSR assistance, in addition to the considerable potential for some countries to act as donors and partners for such assistance in the region. Several countries in the region have fast-growing economies, triggering an increase of middle-class and politically educated populations, along with political demands to carry out reforms and the resources to do so. Some countries in the region are historically large contributors to UN peace-keeping operations, while others would like to follow in their path. Peacekeeping training could thus potentially act as a driver for meeting international standards and initiating discussions on SSG and SSR activities. Moreover, some countries are interested in increasing their international development activities. In addition, there is political will for and commitment to regional experience-sharing, and in areas such as economic cooperation or disaster management, such regional and inter-subregional cooperation has taken place, for instance via the ASEAN+3 and the ASEAN Regional Forum (ARF), the Asia-Pacific Economic Cooperation (APEC), or the East Asia Summit (EAS). Much can be learned from experiences across – and within – Asia with the design, performance, and reforms of countries' security sectors, and the impact and pay-off of such reforms on these countries' peace, stability, and prosperity.

SSR is a politically highly sensitive undertaking. Each country finds its own speed and sequencing in the design and implementation of SSR.

How do SSR and conflict prevention interlink?

The early prevention of the escalation of disputes and tensions to potentially violent conflicts, including through SSR, is a most pragmatic investment in peace and stability. Moreover, in political, economic, as well as human, terms it is much less costly to halt escalating violence than to deal with its consequences. Conflict prevention can mitigate or at least reduce the extraordinarily high human, political, social, and economic costs of violent conflict; it can preserve stability and peace, and it can advance human, regional, and international security and thus secure the foundations for prosperous development and trade (Schnabel and Carment).

Preventive efforts work best if applied as a continuum across all stages of a conflict. Development agencies and both humanitarian and civil society organizations (or security sector institutions) contribute to long-term, structural measures that stabilize societies and their political and economic structures and institutions. However, political actors focus more on crisis diplomacy at advanced stages of conflict escalation. Further along the spectrum of preventive strategies, particularly when initial prevention has failed and tensions have escalated, the deliberate and strategic use of rewards and punishments are expected to bring conflicting parties to the negotiating table – and eventually convince them of the mutual advantages in pursuing compromise solutions. Finally, when there is no consent by the conflict parties, but a sense of an international responsibility to prevent potential grave acts of mass violence or direct threats to international peace and security, third parties including the United Nations and regional organizations may be expected to intervene militarily. Conflict prevention thus ranges from long-term development activities and the promotion of good governance, including in the security sector, to traditional diplomacy, and from crisis diplomacy to more forceful and intrusive forms of preventive interventions.

State governments hold the main responsibility for efforts to prevent disputes from escalating into violence. Actors above and below government levels put pressure on political elites and encourage and empower populations to demand democracy, transparency, and accountability. In that regard promoting good governance is key to the constructive transformation of conflict and the prevention of violence. External support plays an important role in triggering, facilitating, and maintaining local and regional initiatives until those are self-sustaining. Here the United Nations, regional organizations, individual foreign ministries and development agencies, as well as international nongovernmental organizations play a crucial role in encouraging and financing local and national initiatives.

In a study carried out as part of the background research to support the 2017 World Bank/UN study *Pathways for Peace: Inclusive Approaches to Preventing Violent Conflict*, security sector reform

> is seen as a means of progressively building resilient security and justice systems while addressing many of the root causes and drivers of conflict that stem from ineffective, poorly managed, or unaccountable security and justice institutions. Security and justice institutions are commonly the primary interface between the state and the population they are meant to serve. In many contexts they are the litmus test for the effectiveness of the state. Their protracted ineffectiveness or poor integrity represent potential for the escalation of conflict.
>
> (DCAF 2)

The report further argues that

> there is an opportunity to build on examples of the application of SSR principles that have demonstrated an indispensable role in preventing violent conflict and addressing the underlying drivers of conflict. As demonstrated in the case of SSR processes [in many countries where SSR activities have taken place], a sustained,

comprehensive and integrated SSR approach significantly contributes to conflict prevention in times of transition.

(DCAF 2)

SSR plays an important role for measures that – in combination or by themselves – can help reduce the main forces of violent conflict. These measures include the support for democratic transition and consolidation; support in establishing legitimate, representative, and inclusive government authorities; building professional and accountable security institutions; prevention of state-sponsored or -tolerated human rights abuses; and ensuring that the ethnic composition of the security institutions mirrors the population at large. Measures also include the sufficient and broad provision of public services; stabilization of the national economy, including the creation of a stable, transparent, and non-discriminatory environment for private sector development and investment; and trade liberalization and uniform economic development along ethnic lines; resolution of long-standing inter-group grievances, including armed ones, and facilitation of reconciliation; and the prevention of human flight and the creation of an attractive environment for local talent and expertise. All these are important preventive measures in their own right, but also in combination with SSR. The measures contribute to the promotion of good governance, by promoting accountability, transparency, inclusiveness, responsiveness, effectiveness, efficiency, and rule of decent law.

The concept of SSR emerged from the security and development debate. Having evolved in the late 1990s from experiences in fragile post-conflict contexts, it was based on the recognition that reforming a country's security sector and putting security institutions under civilian control are important contributions to and requirements for peace, stability, and long-term prevention of violent conflict. These, in turn, are prerequisites for sustainable economic and human development. While SSR's important role was not recognized in the Millennium Development Goals, it was recognized in the World Development Report 2011 on "Conflict, Security and Development" (World Bank) and of course in the United Nations' Agenda 2030 (particularly Sustainable Development Goal 16 on "Peace, justice and strong institutions").

Switzerland's commitment to building SSG and SSR capacity around the globe and the relevance for China's Belt and Road Initiative

In the context of this joint Chinese and Swiss effort to explore opportunities for conflict prevention, it is worth noting that Switzerland has for decades been committed to promoting conflict prevention through capacity building in security sector governance. Almost 20 years ago Switzerland initiated the creation of DCAF – Geneva Centre for Security Sector Governance, in order to offer non-partisan support to efforts by national and international actors to bring security sectors around the world closer in line with good governance principles.

Throughout this volume, contributors, particularly the Chinese contributors, point to China's various new initiatives in international relations, including its Belt and Road Initiative (BRI). The BRI aims to improve regional cooperation on a trans-continental scale, by strengthening infrastructure, trade, and investment links between China and some 65 other countries covering Central, South, and Southeast Asia, the Gulf countries, North Africa, and Europe. While the BRI aims to bring lasting prosperity and peace to the countries benefiting from the initiative, a welcoming environment for regional cooperation, development, trade, and economic investment *already requires* a significant level of peace and stability. Investments made in the context of the BRI will only last if and as long as basic stability and security are enjoyed by participating countries. Many of these countries, however, suffer from weak security sector governance, which features prominently among the causes of instability, conflict, and violence. Thus they are in dire need of SSR. As this chapter argues, investments made towards better functioning and increasingly accountable security sectors, backed by populations who trust their security institutions, will address some of the causes of tension and help prevent potential escalations to violent conflict. Investments made in SSR are thus complementary to the BRI's investments in infrastructure, trade, and development. The returns on meaningful SSR will be felt by the affected populations, their governments, neighboring nations, and China. The BRI would thus not only bring development, jobs, and wealth to its participating countries, but also increased peace, stability, and order. Moreover, the BRI could offer a highly useful platform for cross-national and inter-regional experience-sharing on SSR.

Given Switzerland's expertise in SSR support and China's interest in stable and prospering BRI participating states, the BRI could serve as a vehicle to promote good security sector governance throughout the BRI community, possibly as a joint Chinese–Swiss initiative.

Conclusion: investing in SSR as a means to support conflict prevention and building sustainable futures

SSR makes sense in its own right, as it improves the delivery of security services and accountability of security providers. SSR reduces the likelihood for security institutions becoming a source of insecurity. SSR builds their capacity to effectively mitigate threats to people's security and prevent the violent escalation of disputes. Investments in SSR are simultaneously investments in conflict prevention, and they improve security and stability domestically and regionally. As well, investments in SSR in neighboring regions are always investments in one's own security.

In sum, SSR is vital for conflict prevention, and both are vital for stability, which is a key ingredient for successful regional cooperation, business, and development. Matching Switzerland's experience in providing SSR support with China's interest in preventing violent conflict and advancing peace through development as part of BRI would be a win–win situation for everyone involved: Switzerland would be able to lend non-partisan support to meaningful, context-specific SSR initiatives throughout China's numerous BRI projects; China would promote and support these activities in order to create a stable environment for development and investment; and the affected societies would benefit from a more effective and accountable security sector and long-term, sustainable conflict prevention and economic development.

Acknowledgment

The author is grateful to Youngchan Kim and Courtney Fung for providing very helpful comments and suggestions on the draft version of this chapter.

Bibliography

Aguja, Mario, and Albrecht Schnabel, editors. *Security Sector Governance in Transition Societies: Working Towards Effective and Accountable Security Provision.* Background Brief for the 14th Inter-Parliamentary Forum on Security Sector Governance in Southeast Asia (IPF-SSG) in Nay Pyi Taw, Myanmar, 05–07 Dec. 2017, Geneva Centre for the Democratic Control of Armed Forces (DCAF), 2018.

Council of the European Union. "EU Concept for ESDP Support to Security Sector Reform (SSR)". EU Documents 12566/4/05, 2005.

DCAF (Geneva Centre for the Democratic Control of Armed Forces). *The Contribution and Role of SSR in the Prevention of Violent Conflict.* DCAF, Apr. 2017.

Donais, Timothy, editor. *Local Ownership and Security Sector Reform.* LIT Verlag, 2008.

European Commission. "A Concept for European Community Support for Security Sector Reform: Communication from the Commission to the Council and the European Parliament". SEC, 2006.

Hänggi, Heiner. "Security Sector Reform". *Post-Conflict Peacebuilding: A Lexicon*, edited by Vincent Chetail, Oxford UP, 2009, pp. 337–349.

Hänggi, Heiner, and Vincenza Scherrer. "Recent Experience of UN Integrated Missions in Security Sector Reform: Review and Recommendations". *Security Sector Reform and Integrated Missions*, edited by Heiner Hänggi and Vincenza Scherrer, LIT Verlag, 2008, pp. 3–4.

Nathan, Laurie. "No Ownership, No Commitment: A Guide to Local Ownership of Security Sector Reform". GFN-SSR, U of Birmingham, 2007.

OECD/DAC. *Handbook on Security System Reform: Supporting Security and Justice*. OECD, 2007.

Schnabel, Albrecht. "Ideal Requirements versus Real Environments in Security Sector Reform". *Security Sector Reform in Challenging Environments*, edited by Hans Born and Albrecht Schnabel, LIT Verlag, 2009, pp. 3–36.

———. "The Security-Development Discourse and the Role of SSR as a Development Instrument". *Back to the Roots: Security Sector Reform and Development*, edited by Albrecht Schnabel and Vanessa Farr, LIT Verlag, 2012, pp. 29–73.

Schnabel, Albrecht, and David Carment. "Conflict Prevention: Concept and Application". *Dimensions of Peace and Security: A Reader*, edited by, Gustaaf Geeraerts, Natalie Pauwels, and Eric Remacle, PIE Peter Lang, 2006, pp. 253–277.

United Nations. "Maintenance of International Peace and Security: Role of the Security Council in Supporting Security Sector Reform – Concept paper prepared by the Slovak Republic for the Security Council Open Debate". UN Doc. S/2007/72, 9 Feb. 2007.

———. "Securing Peace and Development: The Role of the United Nations in Supporting Security Sector Reform". *Report of the Secretary-General*, UN Doc. A/62/659–S/2008/392, United Nations, 3 January 2008.

———. "Transforming Our World: the 2030 Agenda for Sustainable Development". A/RES/70/1, 21 Oct. 2015, https://sdgs.un.org/2030agenda.

United Nations Development Programme. *Human Development Report: Deepening Democracy in a Fragmented World*. Oxford UP, 2002.

World Bank. *World Development Report: Conflict, Security and Development 2011*. https://openknowledge.worldbank.org/bitstream/handle/10986/4389/9780821384398_overview.pdf.

World Bank and United Nations. *Pathways for Peace: Inclusive Approaches to Preventing Violent Conflict*. World Bank and UN, 2018, doi:10.1596/978-1-4648-1162-3.

Wulf, Herbert. *Security Sector Reform in Developing and Transitional Countries*. Berghof Research Center, July 2004.

10 "A community of shared future for mankind" and implications for conflict prevention

Guihong Zhang

Introduction

The concept of "a community of shared future for mankind" is not only the top-level design for China's diplomacy in the new era, but also the Chinese proposal to address global challenges. The new concept inherits the fundamental principles and spirit of the Charter of the United Nations, on the one hand, and provides a new approach to tackle new threats in the globalized world, on the other. The cooperation between China and the United Nations to jointly build a community of shared future for mankind is significant for the prevention of conflict. While to achieve the goal of universal peace and common development through a new type of international relations is the fundamental way to prevent conflict, the co-construction of "One Belt and One Road" will bring strong momentum for developmental peace.

Background

In October 2017, the political report of the Nineteenth National Congress of the Communist Party of China (CPC) mentioned the idea of "a community of shared future for mankind" six times, pointing out that "the Chinese people are willing to work with the people from the rest of the world to promote the construction of a community of shared future for mankind and create a better future for mankind" (Xi "Secure a Decisive Victory"). The Nineteenth National Congress of CPC also confirmed that a community of shared future for mankind is an important component of President Xi Jinping's thoughts on socialism with Chinese characteristics for a new era and the main goal of the major-country diplomacy with Chinese characteristics. The concept was also included in the new Constitution amended in March 2018.

The concept of "a community of shared future" has guided China's diplomacy in recent years in several ways. First, China has made great efforts to promote the regionalization of "a community of shared future" by building up "a community of shared future" with ASEAN, Africa, Latin America, Arab countries, etc. Second, China has provided even stronger support for UN-centered multilateralism. Besides being the second largest contributor to both the UN's regular and its peacekeeping operations budget, China also established the 1 billion USD China–UN Peace and Development Fund and the 3 billion USD South–South Cooperation Fund, and donated to several UN agencies to support UN peacekeeping operations and the development agenda. Third, China has made use of the opportunities of hosting summits (to include the G20, BRICS, and APEC, among others) to integrate the concept into the norms and agenda of these international organizations.

The case of the South China Sea indicates how China tries to prevent conflict by building a community of shared future. A community of shared future in the South China Sea is a part of such a community between China and ASEAN, or more broadly in Asia. China calls for a South China Sea of "peace, friendship and cooperation" through the enforcement of the Code of Conduct in the South China Sea. China also proposed a principle of "shelving the differences and seeking joint development" and a dual-track approach to solve the dispute by political and diplomatic means. To China, the best and the only way to prevent conflict in the South China Sea is to construct a community of shared future based on the existing regional and subregional cooperation mechanism including the China–ASEAN Summit (10+1) and the China–ASEAN Free Trade Area.

However, some major powers and neighboring countries still have doubts about how China would build a community of shared future, given the fact that China has strategic competition with the United States, political stalemate with Japan, and an ongoing territorial dispute with India. In addition, questions remain on how this very Chinese concept can be accepted by international society and transformed into an internationally recognized norm and value.

A community of shared future for mankind is the inheritance and progression of the Charter of the United Nations

The Charter of the United Nations is the cornerstone of a community of shared future for mankind and the basis and starting point for the prevention and resolution of conflicts. In accordance with the Charter, the United Nations has four purposes, along with seven principles. To build a community of shared future for mankind, China advocates the idea of global governance featuring extensive consultation, joint contribution, and shared benefits; the idea of a new type of international relations with mutual respect, fairness and justice, and win–win cooperation, as well as the idea of neighborhood diplomacy including amity, sincerity, mutual benefit, and inclusiveness. These ideas are both the inheritance of and the development of the purposes and principles of the Charter, and are also of great significance for the prevention of conflicts.

When the United Nations was founded, the main problems facing the international community were colonial dominance and the conflict and wars among countries. Since then, the Cold War between the East and the West, the North–South gap, hegemonism, and power politics have become sources of major challenges and conflicts. Accordingly, the Charter sets out the basic principles governing international relations, such as sovereign equality, peaceful settlement of international disputes, and non-interference in internal affairs of other countries. Today, the international community is facing new crises such as finance, environment, refugees; new threats including terrorism, climate change, infectious diseases, cyber security; and new challenges of populism, social fragmentation, and religious antagonism. The idea of a community of shared future for mankind provides China's wisdom and solutions for the international community to deal with these new crises, threats, and challenges.

For example, in the global governance approach advocated by China, extensive consultation means mutual respect, brainstorming, considering the interests and concerns of all parties, thus embodying the wisdom and creativity of all parties; joint contribution means giving play to different advantages and capacities of each other so that all countries can build cooperation platforms and address global challenges together; shared benefits means bringing more cooperation fruits in a fairer way to all peoples and helping to build a community of shared interest, a community of shared destiny, and a community of shared responsibilities.

Another example is the new type of international relations featuring cooperation and win–win situations as not only suitable for the economic field, but also widely suitable for political, security, cultural, and human rights fields. Cooperation is utilized to achieve win–win results to replace the approach of "the winner takes all", aiming to resolve disputes through dialogue and resolve divergence with consultation. Realizing cooperation and win–win results through consultations, contribution, and shared benefits is beneficial in significantly avoiding the occurrence, escalation, or spread of conflicts.

A community of shared future for mankind is highly compatible with the cause of the United Nations

A community of shared future for mankind consists of a community of shared security, a community of shared development, and a community of shared human rights, which are at the core of the cause of the United Nations. As can be seen from the Charter, the United Nations and a community of shared future for mankind share common ideas and thoughts, principles and norms, spirit and values. The maintenance of peace, the promotion of development, and the protection of human rights are the goals of the cause of the United Nations and also the pillars of a community of shared future for mankind. Since its founding, the United Nations has taken measures like preventive diplomacy, mediation, conciliation, political negotiations, and the international rule of law to avoid the occurrence and escalation of conflicts. The Security Council was established to strive towards a community of shared security across the globe.

The promotion of development has increasingly become the focus of the work of the United Nations, and the development system is a part of the United Nations system with widest functions and most institutions. The United Nations, by implementing the four ten-year international development strategies, promoting the Millennium Development Goals (MDGs) and formulating the 2030 Agenda for Sustainable Development, has made major achievements in eradicating poverty, combating climate change, and promoting sustainable development. Safeguarding human rights is also one of the main objectives of the United Nations. By formulating international legal documents for human rights, establishing specialized institutions for human rights affairs and promoting human rights, the United Nations promotes and safeguards human rights, staying committed to building a community of shared human rights across the globe.

Universal security and common development proposed by a community of shared future for mankind is a fundamental way to prevent conflict

Universal security and common development is the basic path for building a community of shared future for mankind and the fundamental way to prevent conflicts. The United Nations is committed to the goal of sustainable peace through conflict prevention, peacekeeping, peacebuilding, and other peace operations. Peace operations are not only the primary means of conflict management by the United Nations, but also the major manifestation of global security governance, and thus remain a public security product for the international community. In today's world, security issues are characterized by inter-connectivity, trans-nationality, and diversity. Only by adhering to cooperation and co-building can lasting security be realized. China advocates a view of global security featuring commonality, comprehensiveness, cooperation, and sustainability, and builds a sense of cooperation to deal with security challenges. To jointly construct a community of shared future for mankind featuring universal security is a Chinese solution for global security governance and an effective way to achieve sustainable peace. Universal security means not only the security of the rich, the strong, and the majority, but also the security of the poor, the weak, and the few.

Common development is an effective way to realize sustainable development. In September 2015, the United Nations Development Summit adopted the 2030 Agenda for Sustainable Development as a guiding document for global development governance and international development cooperation. In recent years, China has actively advocated the idea of common development by hosting the G20 summit, the BRICS summit, and the APEC leaders' informal meetings. In promoting the construction of the Belt and Road Initiative (BRI), the establishment of the Asian Infrastructure Investment Bank (AIIB), the implementation of neighborhood diplomacy and foreign aids, China takes common development as the guideline for its actions. To build a community of shared future for mankind featuring common development is a Chinese solution for global development governance and an effective way to achieve sustainable development.

However, we need to analyze the nature of development and the way to achieve development goals. Only inclusive and sustainable development is the key to conflict prevention. In some countries, exploitation of resources and degradation of the environment as the result of development leads to a lot of turmoil. In other countries, the wide disparity between rich and poor, and the injustice of wealth distribution in the process of development arouse much social disorder. In some cases, slow and gradual development is more appreciated, and too quick and too much development brings social instability. So, it is the development model, not development itself that has much to do with conflict or peace.

Statistics may indicate that richer countries are more stable and have less conflict than those poor countries, but it is hard to conclude that poverty itself will lead to more conflicts. In Southeast Asia for example, GDP per capita in Laos and Cambodia is much lower than that in Indonesia, Philippines, and Thailand, but it is clear that there are more conflicts in the latter three countries. The same phenomena exist in South Asia between Bhutan and Sri Lanka. In those countries with

more conflicts, social problems such as minority separatism, ethnic independence, and religious divergence may have more links with conflicts.
So, it is the root of poverty and the social problem behind poverty, not
poverty itself, that brings more conflicts.

China will make great contributions to preventing conflict by working with the United Nations to promote the new type of international relations

The cooperation between China and the United Nations is a new way to
promote the new type of international relations, jointly implement BRI,
and build a community of shared future for mankind. If a community
of shared future for mankind is the goal, then the new type of international relations is the mode, and the implementation of BRI is the
pathway. The new type of international relations is a new concept and
new thinking offered by China for dealing with new changes in the international layout, new challenges in the international community, and the
new reforms in the international order.

The new type of international relations is to persist in win–win
cooperation and oppose zero-sum games. The new type of international
relations is "to replace confrontation with cooperation and replace
monopoly by win-win" (Wang). Common interests are the foundation and condition for achieving win–win cooperation, and the United
Nations is the main platform and mechanism for member states to
realize the common interests for mankind, such as peace, development,
and human rights.

The new type of international relations is to adhere to multilateralism and oppose unilateralism. The United Nations is the product
and embodiment of multilateralism. Today, the United Nations is at
its time of greatest need to strengthen multilateralism to address global
challenges like terrorism, climate change, and the threat of nuclear proliferation. China is a natural partner of the UN-led multilateralism.
Cooperation between China and the United Nations can provide a
powerful impetus for multilateralism.

The new type of international relations is to insist on the political
settlement of international conflicts and oppose the use or threat of
use of force. Political means should be the main option for resolving
international conflicts. The case of Iraq and Iran proves from both
positive and negative aspects that seeking common ground and convergence of interests of all parties based on multilateral negotiations
and consultations and considering the security concerns of the parties
concerned is conducive to the settlement of the disputes. In contrast,

unilateralism and military means, even if they achieve temporary results, cannot resolve the root of security problems. China persists in resolving major international issues through peaceful negotiations and cooperation within the framework of the United Nations, opposes any unilateral military action that circumvents the United Nations, and discourages member states from easily adopting coercive measures such as sanctions and embargoes.

The new type of international relations is to adhere to the democratization and rule of law in international relations and the opposition of power politics and hegemony. The United Nations advocates the ideas of just security and fair development, promotes the legal settlement of international disputes, standardizes state behavior, restricts state power, and balances national interests by the rule of law, to promote the rule of law in international relations. Power politics and hegemonism are the main factors hindering democratization and the rule of law in international relations, as well as an important source of inequality and irrationality in the international order. As the largest developing country, China is the beneficiary and promoter of the democratization of international relations. In the process of upholding win–win cooperation, multilateralism, political settlement of international disputes, and democratization and rule of law in international relations, China and the United Nations have tremendous room for cooperation to jointly construct and lead the new type of international relations.

China will cooperate with the United Nations to implement the Belt and Road Initiative, which will provide a powerful momentum for developmental peace

President Xi Jinping elaborated on the idea of such a community on many international occasions, including key speeches at the United Nations. The first speech was in September 2015 when President Xi attended the general debate of the 70th session of the General Assembly at United Nations Headquarters in New York to deliver an important speech entitled "Working Together to Forge a New Partnership of Win-Win Cooperation and Create a Community of Shared Future for Mankind" (Xi "Working Together"). The second speech was in January 2017 when President Xi delivered an important speech at the United Nations Office at Geneva entitled "Work Together to Build a Community of Shared Future for Mankind" (Xi "Work Together"), thereby fully explaining to the international community the concept of a community of shared future for mankind. After the vision of a community of shared future for mankind was put forward, it has been enshrined in the relevant resolutions of the UN General Assembly, the Security Council and the Human Rights Council several times (A/RES/72/27; S/RES/2344(2017); A/HRC/RES/34/4; E/CN.5/2017/2). In 2016 and 2017, the UN Security Council and the UN General Assembly respectively adopted resolutions calling for strengthening regional cooperation to provide a safe and secure environment for the implementation of BRI (S/RES/2274(2016); A/71/9).

The cooperation between China and the United Nations to jointly implement BRI is conducive to the overall advancement of the Initiative, upgrading it into an international development agenda. The cooperation between China and the United Nations in implementing BRI can be first reflected in its connecting with the United Nations 2030 Agenda for Sustainable Development. The implementation of BRI should be guided by the new development agenda, so that BRI can be a new model of international development cooperation and global development governance. In particular, with the guidance and assistance of the United Nations development system, the projects and measures of the BRI should be linked up with the development plans of the regional, national, and local governments along the route to germinate and grow.

Second, BRI implementation should not be limited to economic, trade, and investment projects, but also includes many cultural, educational, scientific, and health and other exchange activities, which requires cooperation with United Nations subsidiaries and specialized agencies, so that projects and actions with universal value and global significance can be carried out professionally and locally.

Third, the South–South Cooperation advocated by the United Nations and BRI advocated by China can be complementary and mutually supportive. On one hand, BRI provides the impetus for new South–South Cooperation; on the other hand, the South–South Cooperation will provide a multilateral framework for BRI. The implementation of BRI will effectively strengthen, deepen, enrich, and bring innovation to South–South Cooperation, while South–South Cooperation can also provide experience for BRI to transform itself from a Chinese initiative to a new mode for South–South Cooperation.

Conclusion

As the main goal and top-level design of Chinese major power diplomacy in the new era, the idea of "a community of shared future for mankind" proposed by President Xi will undoubtedly have implications for world peace and security. Yet, the so-called Chinese idea/solution needs to be integrated with existing international principles and norms, and/or transformed into the new ones. China has greatly contributed to UN peacekeeping operations in the last 30 years. However, China's contributions in terms of peacekeepers and finance are yet to be translated into China's higher status and more influence in decision-making and management of UN peace operations. Compared to peace-keeping operations, China invests less and remains low profile in conflict prevention and peacebuilding. "A community of shared future for mankind" provides a future direction for the prevention of conflicts from a Chinese perspective. But, more importantly, how to transform the idea of this community into international norms and values serving for conflict prevention is a common challenge for both China and the rest of the world.

Bibliography

"Joint Communique of the Leaders Roundtable of the Belt and Road Forum for International Cooperation". Belt and Road Forum, 16 May 2017. www.beltandroadforum.org/english/n100/2017/0516/c22-423.html.

United Nations. "UN Charter (Full Text)". www.un.org/en/sections/un-charter/un-charter-full-text/.

United Nations Economic and Social Council. "Social Dimensions of the New Partnership for Africa's Development". E/CN.5/2017/2, 22 Nov. 2016.

United Nations General Assembly. "Report of the Conference on Disarmament 2017 Session". A/RES/72/27, 22 Sept. 2017.

United Nations General Assembly. "Report of the United Nations Joint Staff Pension Board". A/71/9, 14–22 July 2016.

United Nations General Assembly. "Resolution Adopted by the Human Rights Council on 23 March 2017". A/HRC/RES/34/4, 6 Apr. 2017.

United Nations General Assembly. "Transforming Our World: the 2030 Agenda for Sustainable Development". A/RES/70/1, 21 Oct. 2015.

United Nations General Assembly/ Security Council. "Report of the High-Level Independent Panel on Peace Operations (HIPPO): 'Uniting Our Strengths for Peace: Politics, Partnership and People'". A/70/95-S/2015/446, 17 June 2015.

United Nations Security Council. "Resolution 2274 (2016): Adopted by the Security Council at Its 7645th Meeting, on 15 March 2016". S/RES/2274(2016), 15 Mar. 2016.

United Nations Security Council. "Resolution 2344 (2017): Adopted by the Security Council at Its 7902nd Meeting, on 17 March 2017". S/RES/2344(2017), 17 Mar. 2017.

Wang, Yi. "Build a New Type of International Relations Featuring Win-Win Cooperation". *Study Times*, 20 June 2016.

Xi, Jinping, "Secure a Decisive Victory in Building a Moderately Prosperous Society in All Respects and Strive for the Great Success of Socialism with

Chinese Characteristics for a New Era". Delivered at the 19th National Congress of the Communist Party of China, 18 Oct. 2017, www.xinhuanet. com/english/download/Xi_Jinping's_report_at_19th_CPC_National_ Congress.pdf. Accessed 30 Aug. 2018.

Xi, Jinping. "Working Together to Forge a New Partnership of Win-Win Cooperation and Create a Community of Shared Future for Mankind". Statement by Xi Jinping at the General Debate of the 70th Session of the UN General Assembly, New York, 28 Sept. 2015, www.fmprc.gov.cn/mfa_ eng/wjdt_665385/zyjh_665391/t1305051.shtml. Accessed 30 Aug. 2018.

Xi, Jinping. "Work Together to Build a Community of Shared Future for Mankind". Speech by Xi Jinping at the United Nations Office at Geneva, 18 Jan. 2017, www.xinhuanet.com/english/2017-01/19/c_135994707.htm. Accessed 30 Aug. 2018.

Zhang, Guihong, editor. *China and the United Nations in Global Governance.* Current Affairs Press, 2017.

Conclusion

Future collaborative efforts to prevent conflict

Rachel F. Madenyika and Jason G. Tower

In an increasingly globalized and inter-connected world, violent conflict is more protracted, highly volatile, and resistant to containment within national borders. In some instances, it combines perilously with social media, cyber networks, environmental deprivation, and disease. This project, *"Policy Dialogue on Conflict Prevention"*, highlights that conflict prevention is about making societies resilient to violent conflict, which is achieved by strengthening their local capacities for peace through reinforcing systems, structures, resources, attitudes, and skills at the local, national, regional, and global levels. Much attention is focused on reactive approaches to conflict – rebuilding and resolving – but prevention must hold the same level of importance. It remains insufficient to merely prevent a relapse of war; the international community must make a greater effort to respond to warning signs to pre-empt the eruption of deadly violence (Woocher).

This manuscript is the outcome of a pilot project that sought to foster exchange between Chinese and Swiss researchers on ways of contributing to the ongoing United Nations' and international debate on peacebuilding in general and the prevention of violent conflict in particular. The document is intended to be an in-depth overview of three policy dialogues that took place over a period of two years. The overarching goal of the project was to encourage a sustained dialogue between Chinese and Swiss experts in this field; exploring avenues for enhanced sharing of knowledge and coordination. The scholars' contributions were intended to open the debate and to offer a forward looking exercise that addresses fundamental questions such as: why conflicts should be prevented; whether "mainstream approaches" are still relevant; and how dominant Swiss and Chinese approaches to prevention both converge and diverge.

The UN has responded to the increase in conflict and insecurity throughout the world by acknowledging that peacebuilding needs to take place before, during, and after the outbreak of conflict. This highlights a shift within the UN towards "Sustaining Peace"[1] – a "holistic approach" to the mutually reinforcing linkages between its three pillars[2] – that recognizes the primacy of politics, while also stressing an approach that strengthens the nexus between peace and security, sustainable development, and human rights policies. Together with the peace mandate of the 2030 Agenda for Sustainable Development and in particular Goal 16, these transformative frameworks have reoriented the UN's efforts to sustain peace to accomplish the spirit of the UN Charter. Most recently, the recommendations of the United Nations and World Bank report highlight a global focus on prevention and seek to improve understanding of how domestic development processes interact with security, diplomatic, humanitarian, justice, and human rights efforts to prevent conflict from becoming violent, reviewing systematically what has worked and not worked. Nevertheless, despite the many policies, reviews, and studies, the question of which issues deserve focus, the balance between long-term and short-term action, and the roles of internal and external actors, are still actively being debated. As with any international collective endeavor, continued inclusion of diverse perspectives is fundamental.

China's increasing participation in UN peace operations, both in conflict-afflicted and in post-conflict states, has been notable. As China's involvement in complex and fragile states deepens, dialogue and coordination with key international stakeholders working on prevention of violent conflict is imperative and comes at a crucial moment, as scholars, in particular, are presently considering how to address increasing violent conflict. This project, which brought together Chinese and Swiss scholars over a period of two years was able to provide learning on dominant models of violent conflict prevention, while assisting the scholars to build a stronger understanding of different models being implemented locally, nationally, regionally, and internationally. As such, these dialogues, which provided an open exchange of ideas around prevention, were important and timely.

This volume reviews the state of the conflict prevention field from various lenses and considers norms and political commitments, institutional capacities, and policy options. The international community, academics and practitioners alike, continues to enhance tools for conflict prevention and refine their application. There were four key areas of convergence that resonated throughout this volume and with participants of this project in general. First, although not necessarily obvious, there are similar national commitments to maintaining peace through multilateral means by both China and Switzerland. China illustrates this commitment through its engagement with peacekeeping operations as the largest contributor of personnel, and the second largest financial contributor among the P5, while Switzerland continues to be central to UN mediation, human rights, and peacebuilding efforts. Second, development approaches must be inclusive. The UN–World Bank report questions our long-standing assumption that income growth alone leads to peace. While clearly stating that inclusion matters as much as growth of institutions in ensuring resilience against conflict, the report emphasizes that successful prevention is built on coalitions of various actors, and that policies for prevention need to address grievances around social and economic inclusion. Third, this volume recognizes that development of new, and strengthening of existing, international norms are necessary to guide and inform multilateral action directed towards prevention. Lastly, the authors of this volume acknowledge that focusing on preventive action at local, national, and international levels is conducive for long-term sustainable peace.

This successful project and innovative collection of work highlights the similarities in both states' approaches to addressing and improving efforts to achieve conflict prevention, pointing to the strong potential for future synergies and fruitful Swiss–Chinese collaboration and continued dialogue.

Notes

1 Security Council Resolution 2282 (27 Apr. 2016), UN Doc. S/RES/2282; General Assembly Resolution 70/262 (17 Apr. 2016), UN Doc. A/RES/70/ 262.
2 www.antonioguterres.gov.pt/vision-statement/.

Bibliography

Woocher, Laurence. "Preventing Violent Conflict: Assessing Progress, Meeting Challenges". *United States Institute of Peace Special Report* 231, 2009.

Index

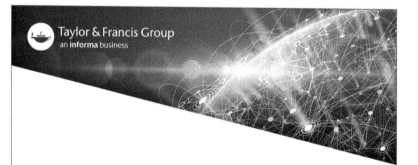